ADVERTISING
Pure and Simple

Hank Seiden

amacom

AMERICAN MANAGEMENT ASSOCIATION

Library of Congress Cataloging in Publication Data
Seiden, Hank.
  Advertising pure and simple.
  1. Advertising.   2. Television advertising. I. Title.
HF5823.S42   1977   659.1   76-41792
ISBN 0-8144-5427-5
ISBN 0-8144-7510-8 pbk

NINTH PRINTING

Foreword

Hank Seiden is one of the few ad men I know who enjoys helping young people get started in advertising. Over the years he has sent me dozens of prospects, although I've always suspected he kept the best ones for himself. Unfortunately, there aren't too many coming along these days. But with this book I expect that will change.

Advertising Pure and Simple is a book I wish I had when I was getting started. A place to learn what advertising is and, maybe even more importantly, what it isn't. Here you'll find examples, good and bad, to illustrate every point along the way. I can't remember when advertising has been spelled out so clearly and advertising myths dispelled so forthrightly.

Don't let anyone tell you this business hasn't changed. At one point in our brief history, Seiden's observations would have earned him considerable scorn and possibly fewer clients. Let's say he would never have been considered for Advertising Man of the Year. But economic vagaries of the recent half decade have awakened the business world. Today, many advertisers and their agencies practice what Hank Seiden preaches. I feel sorry for those who don't.

I don't always agree with Hank Seiden. Especially when he knocks one of the most successful campaigns that Benton & Bowles has ever done. The truth is that commercials the critics blast can still make it big at advertising's box office—the supermarket. Conversely the most lovable advertising (and this always surprises people) can bomb badly.

Picking winners in advertising is still about as scientific as picking hit TV shows. But in this book, Hank Seiden has singled out many winners and, better yet, he explains why they worked.

Anyone who has anything to do with advertising ignores this book at his or her own risk. Anyone interested in getting into advertising had better have damn good connections without this book. Anyone just plain interested in advertising will find this book a fascinating insight into the business.

AL HAMPEL
Executive Vice President
Director of Creative Services
Benton & Bowles, Inc.

Contents

1
A Matter of Conscience

I WROTE THIS BOOK BECAUSE NO ONE ELSE DID.

Too many people—laymen as well as a surprising number of professionals—have been given the wrong impression about advertising largely from books that have been written about this business.

This is not to say that these books may not be useful and/or entertaining, just that they sometimes mislead and often distort. Nor do I mean to imply that many good books have not been written on the subject, each colored, of course, by the author's field of expertise, experience, and point of view, just as this book is. I agree with some and disagree with others.

For simplicity's sake and for the sake of discussion, I have divided the best of these books into several well-defined categories. I think you'll recognize them all.

THE EXPOSÉ BOOKS

These books promise to give a gullible public a keyhole peek at what really goes on behind the closed doors of the clan-destine, mysterious world of advertising. Their authors fall into three specific categories. The first includes the outside debunkers of advertising, the fast-buck feature writers who have done very limited, very questionable, or very preju-diced "research" on the business to stoke the sale of their books. The second category takes in the ex-professionals. They've just left the field (seldom by choice) and they're hungry to make a name for themselves editorially, since their meager talents probably earned them scant acclaim while they were active in the agency business. Books writ-ten by these former insiders tend to be vicious and vindic-tive; with all due respect to women, hell hath no fury like an ad man scorned. These first two categories I call the ad-vertising porno books. They are worthy of no further discussion.

In the third category of exposé books, however, are those written in good conscience by knowledgeable and thought-ful authors. The most important of these are Vance Pack-ard's *The Hidden Persuaders* and Marshall McLuhan's *The Mechanical Bride*, both of which attribute enormous and sometimes sinister powers to advertising. Both these books are worth reading, but since I myself have never been privy to advertising's so-called sinister powers, I take them with several grains of salt.

THE PSYCHOLOGICAL BOOKS

These are the brainwash books. They attempt to show how people can be manipulated by modern psychological tech-niques of advertising into acting against their will. They're scholarly works that make fascinating, if frightening, read-ing. Their authors are not actually advertising practitioners, but are engaged in supportive areas.

For the most part, I find that these books belong more to

the James Bond genre than they do to advertising. They fantasize and complicate what is really a very down-to-earth, simple business. Advertising involves nothing more devious than knowing people, understanding their basic needs, and being able to communicate with them. So books that blame us for sophisticated psychological plots or brainwash devices fall totally short of the truth. The most successful advertising device is still a compelling ad or commercial created by a writer and art director with a feeling for people gained through their own personal experiences in life. Ads like these are not created by psychologists or researchers—thank goodness.

If you read one of these books, and you should, let it be *Motivational Research* by Dr. Ernest Dichter. It's the classic in the field.

THE INSIDER BOOKS

You've probably read one or more of these "advertising personality" books. Autobiographical in form, they shed more light on the author's nature than they do on the nature of the business. If you like light reading that includes a liberal mixture of fact and fiction, you'll be entertained by these. You may also be misled, since they tend to give a somewhat atypical picture of what the business and its people are really like.

These books are not written to be informative. They are written by highly successful, highly competent, and highly interesting advertising people either as a memoir (look for a recently retired author here) or as an effective promotion tool to be used in the pursuit of new business for the author's advertising agency. As such they are intensely subjective, but they make exciting reading.

Four of the most publicized, most enjoyable, and most entertaining are: *From Those Wonderful Folks Who Gave You*

Pearl Harbor, by Jerry Della Femina; *George, Be Careful*, by George Lois; *Me and Other Advertising Geniuses*, by Charles Brower; and *Does She . . . or Doesn't She?* by Shirley Polykoff.

THE TEXT BOOKS

These are the primers usually written by educators. I find these advertising textbooks to be superficial and general in nature, but that's what they're supposed to be. Their purpose is to give the student with no practical experience a quick and general view of the business. As such, they contain more theory than fact, more idealism than pragmatism. But they serve their purpose.

Some, however, suffer from one very serious flaw: though most of them have been recently published or revised, some are antiquated in content, particularly with regard to television advertising, the newest and most pervasive of the media. I was surprised and appalled to discover that most of the textbooks I used 25 years ago are still being used today—and they were old when I used them. That's unforgivable. Is this any way to prepare young people for the advertising profession? Can you imagine that happening in medicine or law?

THE "HOW TO" BOOKS

These are the advertising rule books. They contain rules for everything from headlines to layouts, words, length of copy, typefaces, colors, illustrative techniques, logotypes— you name it, they've got a rule for it. And if they don't, wait a minute and they'll invent one.

Rule books are written by successful people in the field who are dedicated to telling everybody else how to be successful—*their way*. God help the creative person who violates their rules.

These books can be dangerous because they encourage sameness. Rules lead to dull, stereotyped advertising, and they stifle creativity, inspiration, experimentation, initiative, and progress. The only hard and fast rule I know of in advertising is that there are no rules. No formulas. No one right way. Given the same problem, a dozen creative talents will solve it in a dozen different ways. Probably all good.

If there were a surefire formula for successful advertising, everyone would use it. Then there'd be no need for creative people. We could simply program robots to create our ads and commercials, and they'd sell loads of products—to other robots.

If I believed in rules, my number one rule for creative people would be, throw away the rule books—after you've read them. I always make it a rule to know the rules before I break them. Don't knock them, they've worked for some of the most successful people in the field. David Ogilvy's *Confessions of an Advertising Man*; *How to Advertise* by Kenneth Roman, Jr. and Jane Maas; and *Tested Advertising Techniques* by John Caples will give you enough good rules to follow or violate for a lifetime.

Aside from these categories, of course, there are the mechanical books, which get very detailed and specific about the nuts and bolts of the business, like television production or print production, and the specialty books, which spotlight the creation of such specialized advertising and specific media as sales promotion, mail order, direct mail, outdoor, radio, and other sub-specialities.

THE best book I have ever read on advertising, and the one that has had the greatest influence on me, is Rosser Reeves' book, *Reality in Advertising*, published in 1961. This little book contains more wisdom, including the Unique Selling Proposition (USP) theory which is the basis of all solid advertising, than any other book I have ever read. Despite three rather serious drawbacks—it may stifle creativity, it sometimes underestimates the intelligence of the public, and it tends to sound pontifical—if I were asked to recommend only one book on advertising, this would be the one.

I also recommend *My Life in Advertising* (as well as its predecessor, *Scientific Advertising*) by the legendary Claude Hopkins. Though it was written in 1927, much of its theory is surprisingly relevant today. Hopkins was a brilliant, innovative copywriter, considered by many to be the father of copywriting. And he worked for the old Lord & Thomas Advertising Agency, considered by many to be the father of the modern advertising agency. I recommend this book to all who are deeply interested in advertising with two cautions: First, it is egotistically autobiographical. Nobody could ever accuse Mr. Hopkins of having been modest. Second, it is dated in practicality. The world has changed dramatically since Mr. Hopkins' day, most notably because of the bright new world of television, today's most potent medium for the delivery of an advertising message.

Martin Mayer's *Madison Avenue, U.S.A.* is the one other book I consider must reading for anyone who wants to understand the world of advertising agencies. Like the author's more recent books on banking and the legal profession, it is a sober, responsible survey of the advertising business by a gifted reporter. Mr. Mayer looks carefully at the advertising agency rather than the techniques of advertising, and he has written *the* definitive work on the subject.

AND that brings us full circle back to my reasons for writing this book. The world has gotten its impressions of the advertising business and advertising people from books, movies, television, and a few, self-appointed experts within the field. They are probably all wrong.

The advertising business is a tough, demanding taskmaster. The people who labor in it are, for the most part, honest, hard-working, dedicated people who work longer hours under more pressure than almost any other group I know. They've got to be able to work hard because they're in a service business that can lay claim to no tangible product. No factories. No machines. No inventory. Someone once said that an ad agency's inventory goes up and down the elevators twice a day. All we have are people—and their ideas. The people (particularly the creative people) are unusually socially conscious, and they take great pride in the quality of their work. Although the pressure and competition are killing, I have never in my career (contrary to popular belief) worked with an alcoholic. And believe it or not, I know of no one suffering from ulcers, although I know a few clients who do, which may or may not be coincidental.

The people who work in advertising represent the best from all sections of the country, from all schools, and from all social strata. Those from higher income backgrounds, from the Midwestern states, and from white Anglo-Saxon Protestant origins seem to wind up in account-handling capacities, while those from the inner city minority groups find their way into the creative departments. That's a generalization, of course, but an interesting side note. To generalize still further, I find that advertising people—the good ones, anyway—have two traits in common. The first is their intelligence. The second is the unique way in which they approach a problem.

Advertising people tend to simplify problems. I'll prove that right now by stating that there are basically two kinds of people in the world: the Complicators and the Simplifiers. Complicators have wonderfully analytical minds. They're inquisitive. They see ramifications of problems that nobody else sees, endless variations upon a single theme. To them, simple problems become, of necessity, complex. They make great scientists. And lousy advertising people. Simplifiers, on the other hand, have the uncanny ability to grasp a Byzantine tapestry of problems and unrelated facts and come out with the one simple, salient point that links the whole mess together. Simplifiers make lousy scientists but great creative people because they know how to isolate that one most important appeal or feature, and how to communicate it simply. Most good advertising people, on the account and creative sides, solve problems simply.

Aside from their ability to simplify, creative people are just like anyone else, with the same strengths and faults as all of us. With one more exception.

Talent.

All right, you ask, so who *doesn't* have talent? Everyone can write. Everyone has some artistic sense. So everyone is convinced that he or she knows all about advertising and can turn out better commercials than the "junk" he sees on television, right? I don't think there's an ad agency in the world that hasn't, over the years, received a deluge of mail from laymen criticizing its commercials and offering "million-dollar-ideas" for future commercials. Quite aside from the fact that it takes time to answer these letters and that the legal implications relating to unsolicited ideas are labyrinthine, I have never in all my years in this business received, or heard about anyone else receiving, an idea from a layman that could be used. Yet they persist in believing that they can dream up an idea that a battery of creative, trained, talented professionals didn't think of dozens of times and discard. They're not aware of the marketing strategy, the creative objectives, or even the problem. But that doesn't stop them. The letters keep coming. And with each letter comes the conviction that they can create better advertising than the professionals. They're wrong. Hopefully, this book will show them why.

When you take away the exposés, the psychology, the personalities, the textbooks, and the rules, what have you got left?

This book. Advertising. Pure and simple.

Written as a matter of conscience.

2
Advertising: A Realistic Perspective

INCREDIBLE AS IT SOUNDS, AFTER 25 YEARS OF LEARNING, creating, supervising, and writing about it, I really don't believe in advertising. Not as most people conceive of it, anyway.

The popular untruths about advertising are these: It is some weird, mystical science by which a chosen few control the masses. It takes advantage of little-known psychological factors plus the mesmerizing effects of the electronic media to sell us things we don't need and can't afford. It is essentially a refined version of brainwashing that is simultaneously castrating and lobotomizing an otherwise discriminating American public. The way we live, the way we eat, the way we work or relax, even the way we vote can be directly attributed to the enormous power advertising wields. And its potential applications in the future are virtually unlimited.

Nonsense.

The perpetrators of this myth (and it is perpetuated by advertising professionals as well as by laymen) obviously have a very low regard for the basic intelligence of the public at large. After years of trying to sell them what I consider to be sound and useful products, I've seen the public's intelligence at work too many times to deny its existence. And when it comes to an attempt to induce them to part with a buck, I find the Volkswagen crowd at Coney Island to be one hell of a lot more discriminating about spending their hard-earned cash than the limousine crowd on Fire Island.

Just to prove the truth of this to ad people at the outset of their careers, I wish I could force them to do their basic training between these two islands, with refresher courses on an annual basis thereafter. The exercise would go a long way toward destroying the myth of consumer stupidity. Then maybe advertisers would cease to show their contempt for and ignorance of the very people they're trying to sell. And the real truth about advertising could be told: Far from being the ultimate persuasive weapon in the hands of a creative superstar, advertising power is shaped by and subject to the modifying influence of people power. And that's just as it should be.

So what do I believe advertising can do? I believe that a *good practitioner of advertising can convince a logical prospect for a product to try it one time.* No more, no less. Read it again and please pay close attention to the words. I chose them very carefully.

Notice that I use the word "convince." Not badger. Not cajole, intimidate, or fool. To convince requires a rational appeal to another person's intelligence. And we've already verified the existence of intelligence in the buying public.

I said "logical prospect" because advertisers have to learn to be more realistic about their commercial chances than they are at present. A logical prospect is one who is at that moment in time in the market for such a product, has a need for it (or can be shown that he has a need), and can afford to buy it. If you haven't got a logical prospect, your product or service just won't move, no matter how brilliant your advertising is. Cigarettes can't be sold to nonsmokers, for example. Someone who just bought a new car last week is not a logical prospect for your new car campaign. You can't sell a mink coat to a woman who can barely afford a cloth one. It takes desire, need, and capital to make a logical prospect, and there aren't as many of them waiting around to be sold on your product as you might think.

I used the word "try" instead of "buy" advisedly. While it's true that, in most cases, a prospect will have to buy a product in order to try it, I prefer the word try because a trier is a tester while the term "buyer" connotes a steady customer. The best that advertising can hope for is to get a trier, and a one-time trier at that. From then on, the product is on its own. The one-time trier is either going to like the product better than the one he's been using (in which case you've made a new customer), or he won't like it better and will revert to his old brand. In that case, you've lost him until such time as a new improved product is developed together with advertising that convinces him to give it another try. Until then, advertising has done all it can do. It convinced someone to try. *Advertising does not make customers. Only products make customers.*

Let's tread water for a moment.

From 1966 through 1973 I wrote a column called "Storyboard" for a New York-based but nationally influential advertising magazine called *Madison Avenue*. I used my column to criticize (as well as laud) the commercials I saw nightly on my own TV screen. I chose to write about commercials watched at home instead of viewed by invitation in a studio because I wanted to see them in the same environment that a consumer would—with all the distractions of other commercials and programming around them. Also, I believed, and still do, that the only commercials worth reviewing are the ones that run on the air (as opposed to rejects, tests, or commercials done to update creative portfolios). Most of all, I didn't want my reviews to be influenced by knowing which agencies created and submitted which commercials. In most cases, I stuck to this rule so well that I didn't know which agency's commercial I had rapped until I received a threatening letter from its president.

I reached a lot of conclusions about advertising during the eight years I wrote that column. You learn a lot about what advertising can do when you review hundreds and hundreds of commercials, consciously analyzing each one. But most of all, I learned what advertising *cannot* do.

It can't sell a product to someone who has no basic need for it.

It can't sell a product to someone out of the market for it.

It can't sell a product to someone who can't afford it.

It can't make a satisfied customer.

And it can't save a bad product.

If anything, good advertising is bound to have the opposite effect upon a poor product. It'll put the manufacturer out of business. Why? Because the better the advertising, the more people who will try the product. The more people who try the product, the more people who will reject it. The more who reject it, the faster the product will fold. It sounds like a semantic Rube Goldberg machine, I know, but it's true.

When the product flops, two things are guaranteed to

happen. The agency will blame it on the product. The manufacturer will defend his product and attack the advertising. So how can you identify the culprit? By looking at the sales figures, that's how. If the figures indicate a low initial rate of trial followed by a high repeat purchase pattern among the few who *did* try, it's clearly a case of good product/bad advertising. The advertising simply wasn't as good as the product. If it had done its job properly and made enough triers, they would have realized the superiority of the product and repurchased it again and again. Fire the agency.

But if the opposite is true—if a high initial rate of trial suddenly slacks off into a low repeat-purchase pattern, chances are good that a brilliant advertising campaign failed to rescue a poor product. The advertising was too good for the product. It created so many triers for the lousy product that it put the client out of business. Fire the product. An example of this was the original Gablinger's beer introduction. Gablinger's was the first no-carbohydrate beer. It had tremendous appeal and, for the most part, a very good, very dramatic advertising campaign behind it. (See Chapter 6.) The sales figures indicated very high initial trial with virtually nonexistent repeat purchases. You had only to taste the beer to see why. Gablinger's was pulled off the market for many years and has just recently reemerged as, let's hope, a new, improved product.

Again, only products make customers. The best that advertising can do is cause reasonable prospects to try. Once. In a nutshell, that's what advertising can and cannot do. Now that we've defined the ground rules, the rest—how to go about creating an ad—is relatively easy.

The first step, when creating any ad or commercial, is the most critical: Jot down, as two guidepoints, what you're trying to say and the audience you're trying to say it to. If you can't compose one or at most two sentences summing up the key point of your ad, then you're simply not cut out to be an ad writer. Go to bartender school. Learn to tap dance. Become an interior decorator. But please get out of the advertising business! The inability to compose these one or two simple sentences has got to be the cause of much of the confused and garbled advertising I see on TV, in magazines, on billboards. Everywhere I look, it seems, I find an advertising copywriter or art director who didn't really know the one point he wanted to make. An ad or commercial must be single-minded. So an attempt to make three or four points is doomed *a priori* to make none of them.

The creative person must be capable of taking a long, unsentimental look at the audience who is to receive his sales message. Let's assume that you, the copywriter, are taking a bead on a woman (only because women are our biggest customers, particularly in the important area of packaged goods). Let's further assume that she's now using a product in direct competition with the one you want to convince her to try (a logical assumption, by the way, since almost no monopolies exist on the shelves today). Third, she believes for one reason or another that the product she's currently using is the best one she can buy. (Few consumers buy a product because they think it's the *worst*.) Finally we'll suppose that when she runs out of her current supply of the product, she'll purchase the same brand again, more or less automatically—a phenomenon known in advertising lexicon as "brand loyalty."

Now then. Assuming that you truly know what you want to say, do you know your audience well enough to say it as convincingly as possible?

Look at her again—closely, this time. Is that really brand

loyalty you see shining in her eyes? Or is it actually brand *laziness*? Based upon what we all know about most busy women, it seems safe to say that brand laziness is what causes her to buy the same brand repeatedly. Because if there's anything in this world she doesn't need, it's another conflict—the very thing your advertisement is trying to create in her mind.

Friend, she's gonna resist your ad. Her shopping day is a drag anyway, and anything that prolongs it, like niggling doubts about her regular brand, or a temptation to try another, is going to seem about as attractive as cholera. She *knows* she's happy with the product she's using. Her husband is happy with it. Her kids are happy with it. And here comes your damned ad pushing a competitive product ("Try me! I'm better!"), disrupting her complacency, complicating her shopping, and, incidentally, creating a conflict. A minor one, to be sure, but still another irksome conflict.

If your advertising is going to be successful, it had better be strong enough and convincing enough to overcome this brand laziness. That's a tough order, but it can be done with a good, strong, "switching" idea, one that promises the prospect some benefit she will derive from using your product instead of her own, something important enough to make her say, "Hey! I've got to try that" the next time she runs out of her current brand. Can you do it? Sure! Because no matter how passionately they deny it, your prospects are influenced by advertising. Mind you, I don't say they are hypnotized or compelled, but influenced they are, no matter what they say.

But people don't always do what they say they do. Think about it. The first reason a woman usually cites for having chosen a particular brand is its price. It happened to be on sale, you know, and since all brands are alike anyhow, why not buy the cheapest one? Having said that, Mrs. Consumer feels satisfied that she is the compleat wife, an excellent mother, a thrifty homemaker.

But that *isn't* why she bought that particular brand. She really bought that brand just because *she always has*.

You don't believe me? Then prove it: Try to tell the woman who says that all brands are alike that the toothpaste she buys for her children is destroying their teeth—and then duck. She'll leap to the defense of that brand, reciting every reason she ever heard an advertiser give for buying that particular toothpaste. Even if the brand she bought was truly on sale that week, you can bet it was a well-advertised brand bearing a name she has faith in, be it a national or store brand. You couldn't *give* her that toothpaste if she's never heard of it before. No matter how cheap, she won't buy the unadvertised XYZ brand once you have given her a switching idea compelling enough to overcome the few pennies more your product costs.

Go ahead. Give her a switching idea. It's not as hard as you think, because a powerful switching idea is the result of a process so elementary that it's usually overlooked by most ad people: listening to your prospects.

I find focus group interviews with representative groups of logical prospects to be the simplest, least expensive, and most valuable research you can do. Get eyeball-to-eyeball with your customers. Talk to them. Question them. And, most important: listen, listen, listen!

Again, you'll be amazed at how smart, how reasonable, how perceptive they are. When coming up with your switching idea, keep in mind that the objective of almost all advertising today is the winning of "conquest sales" (sales taken from your competitors) —unless your product is one of that fast-disappearing breed which controls a 50 percent or better share of its market. To get the edge on your competitors, you're looking for a switching idea that points out your product's distinctive edge, the factor that separates it from the rest of the herd, that characteristic she's going to recognize even blindfolded.

It's called the *Unique Advantage.*

Every successful product has *got* to have a Unique Advantage. Without it, the advertiser is wasting his money. (Unless he can overwhelm competition simply by outspending everyone, which in itself becomes the product's Unique Advantage.)

But before you can promote the Unique Advantage, you've got to isolate and recognize it in your product. Here are several ways to do so:

1. First and easiest is when the Unique Advantage is inherent in the product itself. It's either visible or otherwise readily identifiable. The advertising must then point out to prospects why this unique feature will operate to their benefit. Not all unique features are obvious advantages. You may have to make this bridge for the prospect.

Polaroid was the perfect example of a product with an inherent and obvious Unique Advantage. The Scripto Tilt-Tip pen of a few years back is an example of a unique feature, the advantage of which was not so immediately obvious. Since we have been a ball-point writing society for so long, I wonder how many of you remember the joy of writing with a fountain pen? You could lean the pen back in your hand at a 45-degree angle and write almost forever without a hint of writer's cramp. Then came the first ball-point pens, which had to be held vertically in an extremely uncomfortable position. Scripto came out with a new kind of ball-point pen in which the point was tilted in the barrel so that *it* was vertical to the paper when the pen itself was held at a comfortable angle. As all ball-point pens improved and became more comfortable, the Unique Advantage disappeared and the Tilt-Tip pen along with it.

2. The Unique Advantage may be difficult to find and, once found, may not be an advantage at all, or may not even be unique at all. Cases like this require a back-to-the-drawing-board attitude and an appetite for hard work. But in an overwhelming majority of cases, something will eventually be found in the appearance, ingredients, use, manufacturing process, packaging, or distribution of a product that offers prospects a compelling reason for trying it. It may or may not be truly unique. So long as no one else is talking about it, it becomes unique to your product by reason of preemption.

An interesting case in point is Snow Crop frozen orange juice. Nothing unique could be found for Snow Crop except that it contained more pulp than the others. Research indicated that it certainly was unique, but that was most certainly not an advantage to about 50 percent of orange juice drinkers. Most people born before World War II liked pulp because their standard of excellence was the freshly squeezed juice thick with pulp. But those born after World War II were weaned on frozen juice from which all the pulp had been removed. They hate pulp and strain it out whenever they find it. Why use a Unique Advantage that strains out half your market? What then? Back to the orange groves.

By careful questioning of the company experts it was learned that various types of oranges grow at various times of the year, each with its own characteristics and taste. The logical question is how is the quality and taste of Snow Crop kept consistent throughout the year. The juice from each of the various types of oranges is frozen and stored, and they are then all blended to a specific formula. This "blend" story became Snow Crop's very successful Unique Advantage. Although all other brands blend too, nobody was talking about it and Snow Crop preempted the claim. It is only now, more than 15 years later, that Minute Maid, using Bing Crosby as spokesman, is selling the same "blend" story after Snow Crop relinquished it.

3. Sometimes the Unique Advantage is in reality a unique disadvantage which, if it can be quickly turned around, will serve the same purpose as a Unique Advantage. I would prefer to have a unique disadvantage in a product I'm working with than to have nothing at all in the product that makes it stand alone. Think of Volkswagen. Think of the way it looks. Would you call its looks an advantage? Its agency did—and convinced a sizable portion of the auto-buying public to think the same. Sometimes a disadvantage is an opportunity in disguise.

Take the classic example that has found its way into all the textbooks on advertising: the tuna fish story. At one time all commercial tuna fish sold was pink. A new company came on the scene with a white tuna—a tremendous disadvantage, wouldn't you say?—in a market used to pink tuna. The white tuna people didn't think so, and advertised their tuna as guaranteed not to turn pink, thereby implying that something was wrong with pink tuna. They made all the other guys see red. How's that for turning a disadvantage into an advantage? They did it so well that all tuna marketed since then is white.

4. Occasionally, no matter how hard you try, nothing unique can be found about a product. It is then the agency's responsibility to recommend the addition of a particular feature to the manufacturer. Or the agency must create a Unique Advantage for the product by repositioning it.

Otherwise, the agency is wasting the client's money. In my experience, there are very few products for which an exclusive claim cannot be made or a new position found. Usually the agency that fails to do this is at fault; it is rarely the fault of the product. There are far more parity agencies than there are parity products.

The Hamilton Beach Butter-up Popper is an example of a Unique Advantage being built into an existing product to fill a need. Home corn poppers had been around for a long time. They all popped corn, and none sold very well until Hamilton Beach recognized that the overwhelming majority of people prefer their popcorn buttered. No popper then on the market turned out buttered popcorn. Just a simple addition to their existing popper did the trick. Since corn pops by heat, they just added a little receptacle at the top of the popper to hold butter, which melts and drips onto the popping corn. Although others have since copied this feature, Hamilton Beach owns the market. The company's only problem is keeping up with the demand.

An example of a Unique Advantage gained by repositioning an old product is Arm & Hammer. Arm & Hammer was always marketed as a baking soda, a fast declining market, until a whole new and much larger market was created by selling it as a refrigerator deodorant. Same product. New positioning. Or take Martinson's extra-fine grind coffee, which was repositioned, with some important product modifications, as the coffee especially made for the new automatic drip filter coffee machines. The fast-growing popularity of these coffee machines represented a tremendous opportunity for a new coffee positioned directly against that lucrative market of heavier-than-average coffee drinkers. The result was a new coffee called "Mr. Automatic." A new need. A new opportunity. A unique new product.

And what will you do with the Unique Advantage once it's been isolated? First of all, it should be tested to make sure the advantage has wide appeal. This is essential because there are no guarantees that a particular unique feature is going to be viewed as an advantage or switching idea by the majority of cash-paying customers. A lemon-flavored mouthwash is a great idea, for example, provided that it can be proved that consumers will find its unique flavor to be advantageous or desirable first thing in the morning.

As for expressing this Unique Advantage in advertising, there's no sweeping generalization that contains a successful formula. I believe in doing what's best for each individual client. I do, however, believe that every ad or commercial should consist of three fundamental ingredients, and that poor advertising can be traced to one, two, or all three of these ingredients being overlooked:

1. Information—about the product and its Unique Advantage.
2. A clear statement of the information.
3. A unique presentation.

If a given ad or commercial contains the first two ingredients (information and a clear statement thereof), you can't possibly have a bad ad. After all, isn't that the definition of advertising—giving information about a product so that people can understand (and, hopefully, desire) it? Wholly of and by themselves, these two ingredients are guaranteed to give you a good ad.

They won't, however, necessarily give you a great one. That's where the third ingredient comes in. Advertising messages are worthless unless they're seen. To make your advertising stand out from the great mass of advertising is absolutely essential for survival today, and that's what this third ingredient is meant to do. It can make your advertising stand out via a unique presentation. Even so, I hasten to point out that a unique presentation alone, without the first two ingredients, is not advertising. It may be art, but it definitely is not advertising. The finest presentation will not cover up the lack of a good, basic selling idea. Similarly, any presentation that gets in the way of or slows down the communication of the idea is not only nonfunctional but counterproductive. Get rid of it.

Occasionally, when discussing these three ingredients with advertising beginners, my audience puts up a wail about the "restrictive nature" of "1-2-3 formulas." They object (sensibly) to discipline that restricts their creativity. I agree, but that isn't the kind of "discipline" I'm talking about here. These three ingredients simply aren't creatively stifling. If anything, they liberate the imagination by giving it a focused headstart in the right direction. What good is undirected creativity? More often than not, it works up a great lather by producing sensational solutions to problems that just don't happen to exist. To be worthwhile, creativity must be directed toward the solution of a particular problem. A writer or art director with these three ingredients in mind stands on a creative springboard from which he can solve the problem of selling his product. I call this *Creative Discipline.*

That's a contradiction in terms, you say. How can creativity be disciplined? I say how can it *not* be and still be advertising?

I check every ad or commercial that goes through my hands for all three ingredients. If it is deficient in any one, it doesn't reach the client. But if it *does* meet these criteria, I find we never have any trouble selling it to a client. More important, it never has any trouble selling the client's product, either.

As for the execution of an ad or commercial, I can't offer any rules or formulas. I have only two words of counsel: *simplicity* (which characterizes all of the very best in advertising) and *believability* (a quality about which you will read more in the following chapters).

The ability to see and present things simply is what makes advertising copywriters a unique breed. I've seen very few fine writers of successful plays or novels who could write good ads. Conversely, I've seen darn few good copywriters who could write novels and plays. They keep trying, but I know they'll never succeed because they're a different breed. (The same holds true for fine painters and art directors.)

Advertising copywriting is an extremely disciplined pursuit requiring a disciplined mind capable of shuffling through stacks of mental index cards until the one precise, correct point to be made is located and extracted. A novelist has 754 pages to tell his story, and if he feels a little rushed, he can make it 755 or 756 pages. An advertising writer or an art director has a 7 by 10 page or 30 seconds of time to get a prospect's attention, tell the story, and try to move him to action. That's tough. For them, the virtue of simplicity is learned during the early stages of their careers out of raw necessity.

As for *believability*, it is simply the single most important word in advertising. If your prospects don't believe what you have to say about your product—no matter how true it may be—your advertisement is worthless. If they do believe you, you have achieved your primary goal.

It is just this—the ability to achieve believability—that separates the advertising professional from the amateur. It makes the difference between a good creative person and what many people think of as "advertising geniuses," but it really has nothing to do with talent. The ability to make yourself believed is intrinsically tied up with a basic liking for people, a willingness to know them, understand them, listen to them, respect them, and, above all, be honest and sincere with them. You can't fake it, because they're just too smart. So tell it to them straight.

And one more thing. Remember, the product is the hero, not the advertising.

You now know everything I know about advertising. And everything I believe in. What follows is merely substantiation.

3
Concept vs. Execution

QUICK! THINK OF THE WORST COMMERCIAL YOU EVER SAW.

Got it? Now then, with the camera eye of your mind, pan in on each loathsome detail, then sweep the screen from left to right, lingering where it hurts most. What do you see? Is it the unctuous spokesman mouthing lines you've heard often enough to repeat in your sleep? Is it a plain, dumpy housewife rhapsodizing about a product you've grown to despise? Or a stomach-churningly explicit demonstration of a nasal decongestant? Choose carefully.

Because chances are you're going to be wrong.

The worst commercial you ever saw was not the one that caused you to throw your shoes at the television screen. The worst commercial you ever saw caused you to laugh, dance, or sing along instead of making a decision to try the product advertised. I'll stake my reputation on that.

The unctuous spokesman, the depressing housewife, or the nauseating demo you associate with the "worst" in advertising probably goads you to fury because most likely it contains no real sales message but hardsells as if it did. It insults your intelligence every second of the way.

These commercials belong to the incorrigible *poor concept, poor execution* category. Don't waste your vitriol on them. They're so bad, they don't even bother me anymore. I just shrug them off like so many annoying gnats. The commercials that really bug me as an advertising man are those in which the sales point gets upstaged or downstaged by the execution.

There are two distinct categories of these, and once you're onto them, you can pinpoint where they go wrong in a minute. The first is what you might call the *good concept, poor execution* commercial. You know the kind: the first sharp stab of irritation it excites dissolves gradually into lingering pity for a sound idea gone awry. Midway through any one of the Heinz "Slowest Ketchup in the North, South, East, and West" commercials, you can feel this phenomenon taking hold as the idiocy of a ketchup bottle dressed up like Howdy Doody in a neckcloth, chaps, and spurs gives birth to a grudging respect for the "slow ketchup" idea. Had they concentrated more upon the ketchup and less upon the Old West, Heinz might have made a valuable and unusual sales point more effectively.

Or how about the *New York Times* commercial that began with this almost perfect concept: "You don't have to read all the news, but it's nice to know it's all there." For a paper that competes with the New York *Daily News* (a summarized condensation of the day's headline stories in an easily handled tabloid form), the *Times* did pretty well in choosing a sales message. After all, depth and breadth is its Unique Advantage, and promoting it in a form that makes it easily digestible is a praiseworthy goal for a *Times* ad. So how did they dramatize this concept on TV? They didn't dramatize it. They merely rolled the slogan (plus some additional copy) past the audience on the screen while an announcer read it off. Period. That isn't television. That's radio. If the concept wasn't actually *killed* by the execution, it was certainly put to sleep. Watching this commercial for the first time, I felt the way I do when I look at the ruin wreaked by an early frost on a windowbox garden—a minor irritation, a sneaking feeling of sadness, and, finally, resignation. It might have been really nice. Not great. Just really nice.

But I can't work myself up into a similar tristesse over commercials in which the execution actually negates the concept. In this second *good concept, poor execution* category, the quality of mercy is strained beyond endurance. A good or even great concept that is utterly destroyed by execution is a perversion of advertising, a self-indulgence on the part of agencies that is part of a frightening and growing trend. To see one of these slick little pieces of hoodwinkery is to watch a so-called professional present his fondest creative dream wrapped in the guise of advertising. Mostly, the execution and the concept proceed to develop independently of one another, almost as if different people were involved at each stage.

Could it be that good creative advertising people are thinking up the initial concepts and then passing them along to production specialists to finish up? It must be. Because it's the production, or rather the overproduction, that strangles the advertising idea in the end. Such production has given birth to an industry that rivals or surpasses the advertising agency business itself, with production houses raking in the dough and their directors becoming the new breed of advertising millionaires.

Obviously, perspective has been lost somewhere along

the way. Were I the client, my agency would have to do one helluva lot of fast talking to induce me to part with more than $35,000 to produce a single TV commercial. In my heart of hearts, I'd prefer to spend $10,000 less than *that*. To wheedle more than $50,000 out of me, the agency would have to show me that my money was absolutely essential to make a brilliant concept come off. I sure wouldn't spend it for show biz effects. More about this is in an upcoming chapter.

What's needed in advertising today—even more than fresh ideas for dramatic development—is a return to what advertising is all about. The basic selling concept, the compelling reason to buy, the unique angle—these are the guts of a commercial and the toughest part to formulate. They're worth their weight in gold and deserve 90 percent of the time spent on the commercial by the agency *and* the client. The remaining 10 percent should be spent on execution, not the other way around. As a matter of fact, the stronger the concept, the less time and effort and money are required for the execution.

Look at the Schaefer beer campaign that ran on TV for over 10 years if you want to know what a great concept looks like. Concept is the result of a creative process, true, but most times, with the really good ones, a marketing fact or statistic will prime the creative pump just a little bit. Obviously that's what happened at Schaefer's agency. They took the fact that 10 percent of the beer drinkers consume 90 percent of the beer and directed the campaign right smack at the heavy users with the slogan "Schaefer is the one beer to have when you're having more than one."

This heavy-user concept does several things. First, of course, it concentrates upon the right audience. Second, it implies that the beer is light, unfilling, and exempt from the law of diminishing returns—that is, several can be consumed with no loss of enjoyment. Finally, it makes drinking more than one beer, or even two or three more than *that*, socially acceptable. It takes a great concept to be able to do all these things, and this one's great. That's why it hurt so much to see the advertising agency that created this great campaign summarily fired and the new agency replace it with an insipid campaign in the tired old soft-drink mold. It pictures all those pretty young people (again!) this time guzzling beer to the uninspired musical theme of something called "We're Schaefer people." It's enough to make you cry in your beer!

Execution, on the other hand, is only the craft we use to express the idea. Far from being an end in itself, it is merely the means to the end. And so, as a rule of thumb, I've learned to be guided by this principle: Any execution that enhances, speeds up, and/or makes more understandable and believable the communication of the basic selling idea is a good one; any execution that slows down, confuses, dominates, or subverts the communication of that concept is dead wrong.

The only thing more annoying than a good concept, poor execution commercial is its opposite, a cotton-candy fribble that looks great, sounds great, and yields nothing when you try to bite into it. This is the *poor concept, good execution* category, a variation on the theme established above. You get a four-star production created by technicians who know their medium, but the concept fails to live up to the execution.

If you ever saw any of the old TWA "Up, up, and away" commercials, you know what I'm talking about. It's a fine song. The special effects are great. The casting is just fine. But what these commercials don't seem to have is an *idea*.

And for a campaign that purportedly won back the straying account for the agency, that's a very serious lack indeed. A campaign, I always thought, should be based on an idea, a concept, a specific goal. The TWA commercials failed to do any of these things—beautifully. What kind of idea is "Up, up, and away"? It's a pop song, isn't it? And one that tells me nothing about TWA, except that TWA planes go "up up and away." If this is the point of the campaign, then TWA is advertising that its planes fly. Well, it's nice to know they do, but that's not what I'd call a smashing advertising concept. I wonder if the same agency would advertise that its food account products are edible?

Visually, these commercials did exactly the right thing: they built up to a point where the copy can step in and deliver the sales punch. Only the copy never showed up. In one example, we were shown quick shots of people scurrying around an air terminal presumably bound for a TWA flight (although we are never actually *told* this). Toward the end of the commercial, each of the people we had met earlier starts running (in emphasis-laden slow motion, no less) for the TWA plane, including the pilot and crew. This is it: the moment when the concept is supposed to step in, neatly intercept the ball, and run it safely to the goal line. But there's no one there. Instead, we hear a sweet chorus of "Up, up, and away" and that's that. Are we told who these people are who fly TWA? The hippie rock band, the lady with a poodle in a Rolls-Royce, or the newly married couple? No, we aren't, so we have no right to conclude that TWA passengers are different from—or representative of—most airline passengers. (The only thing I can gather from this commercial is that TWA passengers are always late, including the crew.) They're just there. Flying. And we're left back on the ground with the taste you get in your

mouth when you bite into an artificially sweetened confec-
tion: an initial shock of pleasure followed closely by an
overwhelming dissatisfaction and then a bitter aftertaste.

Now let's talk about what we *should* be seeing on our
television screens every night—commercials with *good concept*
and *good execution*.

Not too long ago, I had the pleasure of reviewing a few of
the commercials done for the Chesapeake & Potomac Telephone Company by an agency located outside of New York
City. Dramatic, involving, and exciting, without resorting
to even a hint of a gimmick, these commercials all put
execution into its proper perspective. In one, for example,
we are shown a split screen. (The screen is cut in half vertically and two pictures appear simultaneously, one in each
half.) Two young men sit in phone booths calling a girl for a
date—the same girl. One of the boys looks up her phone
number in the telephone directory while the other calls information. The guy who looks up the number himself finds
it, dials it, and starts speaking to the girl right away. At the
same time we see the other kid still trying to get the number
from the information operator. When he finally gets it and
dials it, naturally he gets a busy signal because she's accept-
ing a date from the fellow in the other booth. It ends with
the slogan, "Look it up yourself—it's faster." This is what I
call the simple, believable transmission of a simple idea, and
it proves that a good execution needn't be dull. It just
needs to be clear.

Here's another example, done live, not prerecorded.

This commercial takes as its objective to show—each
time—how easy it is to start the Sears power lawnmower.
Simple. Especially when you consider that the number one
consumer objection to buying a power mower is the complicated procedure of starting it up. Each time the commercial
is run, the announcer makes reference to the show on which

it appears (a half-time score, perhaps, or the show's plot) to demonstrate that the spot is live. Then, carefully noting the number of successes and failures he's had to date, the announcer proceeds to start the mower. The only time I ever saw it miss was on the very first try, but that's beside the point. The real point is the confidence the Sears people have in their product which allows them to take the risk *live*, on a time-after-time basis, that the mower won't start.

I think that's worth a thousand kicking legs and catchy tunes. It's a great concept, and a great execution. I can only hope we'll see more commercials like it instead of questionable demonstrations, extravagant claims, phoney show biz tinsel, and the irrelevant nonsense we've come to accept meekly. A forceful idea put across forcefully to the prospective customer sells the product. Next time you watch a commercial that tries to sell you on the reliability of its product, ask yourself if it succeeds as well as the Sears mower commercial.

And consider this one: an elegant couple is enjoying a very formal dinner in the ornate dining room of a mansion. The doorbell rings. They spring into immediate action, clearing the table and loading all the dishes, glasses, pots, and pans into the dishwasher. Within seconds, they're pressing the machine's starter button. By the time they answer the door, we're on to their secret: This couple is, in reality, the butler and maid employed at the mansion, taken by surprise at the unexpected return of the lord and lady. You can't dispute the fact that it's a great demonstration of how quickly and easily the RCA Whirlpool dishwasher can be loaded, how much it can hold, and, most important, the fact that scraping and prerinsing are unnecessary. These are big points and they're made with a comic execution that's relevant and functional to the sales point. Who says humor can't sell? When it's used like this, it sells very well.

Another fine concept executed with panache underlines a recent 7up "Uncola" commercial. Sporting a leather jacket and a "waterfall" pompadour, and twirling a long keychain, the ghost of a 1950s sharpie reminisces about the great times he had with his gang at the old hangout luncheonette. In particular, he recalls all the colas they drank. As this ghost watches today's kids, he observes that they don't order colas anymore, they drink 7up. In an irresistible fadeout, our hero strolls off into the gathering mist, combing his ducktail into an oleaginous swirl. For pure excellence, this one is hard to beat. Its concept is right on, labeling cola as an old-fashioned drink of the past, while boosting 7up as the "in" drink of today's knowledgeable kids. Who could ask for more? A great concept executed with verve and imagination.

HIGH-CALIBER commercials like these are what we *should* be watching on TV. They are incisive, they are simple, and they don't waste the viewer's time or the client's money. And they're not hard to separate from the crowd. Just look for a commercial that actually *sells* you something, be it oatmeal or a political candidate, by offering you a clear compelling reason for buying, with a believable execution.

When is an execution believable? When it's inseparable from the concept. When it delivers its message unmistakably, yet remains altogether unobtrusive. When it leaves you completely unaware of its existence as a separate entity. When it does not obscure or overpower the message and is functional to the idea. Good execution is most often brilliantly simple and shockingly inexpensive to produce. Believe me, good execution is the best friend a concept can have.

To conduct your own acid test of an execution's worth, try asking yourself objectively whether the execution gets the message across faster, more clearly, and more believably than if a stand-up announcer delivered it. If it does, then the execution you're watching is functional to the sales message and an aid to the commercial. If you must honestly conclude that it does not, that a straightforward pitch would be more believable, then some advertiser is pulling your leg.

Remember: There are no geniuses in the advertising business. *You* are as qualified to judge the merits of a commercial as the man behind the camera, probably more so, if you train yourself to regard a commercial as the sum of its parts.

All commercials fall into one of four categories:

Commercials with bad concepts and bad execution.
   They're the worst.

Commercials with bad concepts and good execution.
   They're almost as bad.

Commercials with good concepts and bad execution.
   They're inexcusable.

Commercials with good concepts and good execution.
   That's advertising.

It's easy. Determine the category and you determine the worth of the commercial.

4

The Making of a Television Commercial

I REALLY DEBATED WHETHER OR NOT TO INCLUDE THIS chapter in this book.

It's not necessary, you know, to understand the ins and outs of television production in order to tell good advertising from bad advertising. If it were, every ex-Hollywood film technician would be an authority on advertising. Lest I scoop my next chapter, let me say only that this just isn't so.

But since so many of the points I make in these pages about advertising are illustrated by commercials, and because most of the production money spent on advertising today is spent on commercials, and because I refer so often to television execution—it might be helpful to know what goes into each brief spot that rolls across your screen each day and night. You may be surprised to know how detailed a process commercial-making is.

The first thing you need to make a TV commercial is a good idea. (You'll find this statement repeated over and over again throughout this book.) A lightbulb has to go on over someone's head before the lights go on on a television stage set and the cameras can start rolling. Usually it's the creative department of the agency that accounts for the wattage. When the copywriter and art director assigned to the account sit down together to thrash out their ideas, they first develop a storyboard—a comic-strip-like device that has a pictorial representation of the commercial drawn in frames, with the words typed below each frame. Usually this creative team will develop quite a few storyboards. From these, the agency chooses the one storyboard that seems to best solve the problem. This one is presented to the client.

Once the client approves the storyboard, it is turned over to the agency producer. As his title implies, he is in charge of producing the commercial. It is his responsibility—and that of his department—to oversee every aspect of the production from start to finish. Costs as well as creative considerations are his worry, and he must balance the two so carefully that neither suffers. When the storyboard reaches the agency producer's office, much of the eventual success or failure of the commercial rests in his hands.

The first thing he or someone in his department does is to submit a photostatic copy of the storyboard to the Continuity Clearance Departments of the three major television networks so they can make certain it meets their standards of truth, fairness, and taste. All the networks require that advertising claims be substantiated with written proof and documentation, but each network sets its own standards of fairness and taste. What one network will accept, another may not. So you can imagine how difficult it is to get a storyboard that all three networks will agree upon. And what was agreed upon one day may well be rejected the next. Without going into detail here (because I'm saving my big guns for Chapter 21, "The Regulation of TV Advertising"), let me just point out that the decisions taken by the networks at this stage can be quite arbitrary, and getting final copy approval can be a *very* frustrating experience. Quite often, it ends in defeat; one network recently reported that over one-third of the storyboards initially submitted to it are rejected for one reason or another!

While the struggle goes on to get the storyboard approved by the networks, photostats of the commercial are sent to a select group of outside TV production companies for competitive bids. Interestingly enough, production companies tend to specialize in various subjects. Some specialize in food, some in people and dialogue, some in fashion. There are production companies that perform better in a studio, just as there are some that are better out on location. Some are very expensive, some less. All of these factors are taken into account when the production houses are asked to bid on the commercial. On the basis of their bids (and the aforementioned creative considerations) a production company is chosen to do the commercial.

All right. The preliminaries are out of the way, and at this point we're ready to attend the pre-production meeting—a gathering of agency, client, and production company to go over every aspect of the commercial and finalize all of the details. This meeting of the minds is crucial, as you can well imagine, to eliminate costly mistakes that might be made on the day of the shooting. The details discussed will include everything from what, exactly, the people in the commercial will wear to what props will be shown in each scene, precisely how long each scene will run, what camera angles will be employed, how the product will be shown or demonstrated, and the myriad other questions that must be answered *before* the camera begins to roll. If the commercial involves actors and actresses, it is at this meeting that final casting selections are made from a list of people who have tried out for the part. Final wardrobe is chosen, final set designs or locations are agreed upon, and the shooting date is set.

And then, the shooting. First off, it isn't cheap. The cost of a 30-second TV commercial today can run anywhere from $6,000 to $80,000, depending on the talent chosen and the complexity of what is to be shot. On the average, a 30-second commercial runs around $15,000.

The people who participate in the shooting of a commercial are highly trained and highly paid. They are not employed by the agency, but are part of the package supplied by the outside production house. The average TV commercial requires the services of these professionals:

The Director. The director is responsible for the overall look and quality of the commercial, so he is involved in every aspect of production, from camera angles to lighting to directing the actors and actresses. A production company is judged by the talent and capabilities of its directors. They are the people agencies rely upon to take the glorious idea on the storyboard and translate it successfully into film.

The Assistant Director (A.D.). As the title suggests, this person is the director's right hand. He generally coordinates the whole commercial and makes sure that everything required for the commercial is there when it's needed. The assistant director is responsible for keeping the production moving smoothly and efficiently. You'd recognize an A.D. by his familiar chant, "Quiet on the set!"

The Cameraman. He is responsible for anything and everything that has to do with the camera. Like making sure that the exposure is correct, the camera is in focus, the correct lens is being used, the camera is functioning properly, et cetera.

The Assistant Cameraman. He assists the cameraman in all

of the above. He's also responsible for seeing to it that there is enough film in the camera and reloading if there isn't. If the camera runs out of film in the middle of a take, you will recognize the assistant cameraman by the smoke curling off his heels as he runs from an irate director.

The Sound Man. Where there is dialogue or other on-camera sound in the commercial, it is the responsibility of the sound man to make sure that it is all properly and clearly recorded. His is the world of microphones and tape recorders. When he does his job well, you don't notice him. But if you can't hear something clearly, or if you see a microphone in the picture that shouldn't be there, you know he's failed. Mostly, though, sound imperfections are corrected long before the finished commercial reaches your television screen.

The Electrician, or Gaffer. This professional makes certain that everything in the commercial is lit the way the director wants it lit. He works with the director and the cameraman to make sure there is enough light for a proper exposure, to eliminate unnecessary shadows, and to enable the viewer to read the name of the product on the box. He also moves cables, prevents blown fuses, and even turns off the lights when the shooting is over.

The Script Girl. The script girl makes sure that everything that is supposed to be shot *is* shot, and that nothing is forgotten. She also times each sequence on the storyboard as well as each "take" to ensure that it is the right length within the overall context of the commercial. In addition, she keeps track of which "takes" should be developed and which should not because of their unsatisfactory quality; she assigns numbers to each "take" to assist the editor later on. When the guy in the movies says, "Take eight" and slams down the sticks, it is the script girl who has provided him with the correct number.

The Grip. This is the man who moves the camera around at the behest of the director, principally so that all shots can be covered with the desired moves and from the desired angles. In general, he helps move anything heavy that has to be moved—like furniture or scenery. The grip is the muscle behind the production.

The Prop Man. You guessed it! He's in charge of all props, makes sure that they're all in good shape and positioned properly for the camera, and that all special props are functioning properly.

The Set Designer. Not only does he design it, but he supervises the building of the set until he's satisfied that it will give the desired effect. If Rome has to be built in a day, it's his worry.

The Make-Up Man, Hair Stylist, and Wardrobe Stylist. It's up to these people to make certain that all the people in the commercial are dressed, coiffed, and made up properly.

The Home Economist. If food is to be shown in the commercial, it is the home economist who prepares it on the scene and makes sure it looks as luscious as possible. More important still, the home economist works to ensure that the food will photograph as luscious as it looks.

So there they are. By working together, these people apply their diverse talents to capturing on film what was originally conceived on a storyboard. When they finish, the next stage of the commercial process can begin: editing.

Editing is done by the *editor*. He's the person whose responsibility it is to take all the film that has been shot and piece it together into the finished commercial to fit the allotted time. He is usually selected (with the approval of the agency) and paid by the outside production company. He works with the director, the agency producer, and the agency creative team.

Editing starts with the viewing of the *dailies,* or *rushes.* The rushes consist of all the film that has been selected to be developed by the script girl—that is, all the "good" takes from the shooting.

At this point the director, the agency, and the editor, working together, separate the wheat from the chaff by selecting the best takes (there are sometimes dozens of different takes for each individual sequence of a commercial) from the raw footage.

Now the editor begins to work his magic. Following the storyboard, he puts the selected takes together to form the first *rough cut* of the commercial. The resultant bit of film is called the *work print.* Believe me, it gets worked and re-worked. The editor may, for example, substitute one take for another to see which works better. Or one scene may be lengthened while another is shortened. A close-up may even be spliced in instead of a long shot to see if it improves the commercial. It's done over and over and over again until a satisfactory work print is achieved.

Since the work print represents only the pictorial part of the commercial, the next step is to concentrate on the audio part. Now all the off-camera voices (announcers, for instance), sound effects, and music are recorded. Each of these elements is laid down on a separate track. Then it is all mixed together into one sound track at a special recording session called, appropriately, the *mix.* At the mix all kinds of subtle adjustments can be made in the sound track. The music can be lowered, for instance, and the voices can be made louder. Sound effects can be raised or lowered. Bass and treble can be balanced. And much more.

From there, it's a simple matter to place the *mixed track* alongside the work print to see how they work together. This means running the separate audio and film tracks simultaneously. This is called the *interlock* stage.

Finally the last stages of production can begin. First, all of the optical effects are put into the film at the optical film laboratory. *Opticals* include things like dissolves (where one scene fades into another), wipes (where one scene is "wiped" off and replaced by another), and special effects (such as things popping on and off the screen and titles). When the opticals are in, you've got a *slop print*. It's now time to put the film portion and the sound portion of the commercial together.

Film people know this as the *answer print* stage. It's the first time that all the elements of the commercial (completed picture and sound) are joined on one piece of film. This print is corrected for color and overall balance so that some scenes do not appear too dark while others appear too light. When a satisfactory answer print comes out of the laboratory, the production process is all but complete.

There remains only one last thing to be done. Since most commercials are produced on 35mm film (for best quality) and most TV stations are equipped for 16mm film, the 35mm answer print is duplicated in quantity on 16mm film. Individual *release prints* are then sent to each network or station.

This entire production process, from start to finish, normally takes about six weeks. So what happens when you don't have six weeks to complete a commercial?

Videotape.

There are two primary advantages of Videotape. The first is that you don't have to wait for film to be developed in a laboratory, but can play back what you've shot instantaneously. You've seen this done if you've ever watched an "instant replay" on a TV sports event.

The other advantage to Videotape is that it can be edited electronically (and again, almost instantaneously) to include certain basic effects. It all adds up to a great saving in production time, though you still have to allow the same amount of time for pre-production and shooting. It is not impossible—though it is somewhat unusual—to shoot a commercial on Videotape one day, edit it that night, and have it on the air the following day.

So why doesn't everyone use Videotape all the time?

Simple. While the cost of Videotape and film today are pretty much the same, Videotape has some big drawbacks. The "look" of Videotape is noticeably different from that of film. It's harsher. Starker. In many ways, it's colder and more clinical than film, which means that it's sometimes less dramatic and less flattering than film. Moreover certain sophisticated optical effects are impossible to achieve on Videotape. And finally, it's less flexible than film; what the camera sees on Videotape is basically what you get. It's easier to make changes on film.

All this is to say that both film and Videotape have their advantages, disadvantages, and outspoken adherents. Each does its job a little bit differently, but each, when used properly and for the right reasons, can do its job very well indeed.

So now you know what goes into the making of a commercial. To find out what makes a commercial into *advertising*, read on.

5

Show Biz vs. the Advertising Business

I DON'T KNOW HOW PRIME TIME PROGRAMMERS FEEL ABOUT this, but for the advertiser, television is a beautiful but unruly beast. If approached correctly, it can enhance his commercial and sell his product as no medium has ever done before. Mishandled, it will devour the advertiser and his message and purr over the remains of his commercial. Just don't try to tell this to the creators of your favorite "funny commercial." They're way too busy writing one-liners to notice that they're being eaten alive by their pet medium.

Commercial funnymen don't *want* to think that they're stepping on the beast's tail by turning out commercials that are 99 percent show business and 1 percent advertising. They want to think they're advancing the cause of creative advertising a couple of millennia for every sight gag they write. The more medium they apply, the less message we get, but your true technical virtuoso doesn't like to think about unpleasant realities. So long as some sponsor is willing to foot the bill for his creative fantasies, he's going to sugar-coat the sales message with as many layers of entertainment as it will hold. And if he's lucky, maybe he'll win an advertising award for it, too.

To revert back to a previous chapter, if I had to choose between two extremes to advertise my product, I'd choose a commercial that offered a great selling idea wrapped in a pedestrian execution rather than the other way around. Because it's the selling idea that's at the heart of advertising, for better or worse, however effective or ineffective it might be. Without a selling idea, you have nothing that even resembles advertising—only a film clip belonging to some entertainment archive somewhere far away from the advertising agency. The client doesn't mean to be a sponsor of the arts. He's paying his agency for advertising, not entertainment. He wants us to sell his products and ideas, to devise new and compelling reasons for people to buy his goods. His money supports our creativity only as it applies to thinking up new appeals to his logical prospects. That's what advertising people are paid for. And lately we've been highly overpaid because we're not in the advertising business any more. Too many of us are in show biz.

Look at what some of our extravaganzas cost. Computed on a per-minute basis, they exceed the costliest cast-of-thousands Hollywood epic, making them look like shoestring operations. The $100,000 commercial is not unheard of, even though it should be. And not too long ago, an agency bragged within my hearing about the $200,000 commercial they'd just produced. At that rate, a two-hour feature would cost $24 million.

But then, who's crazier, the frustrated Fellinis who create these monsters or the clients who pay for them?

I'm not advocating the kind of commercials that put you

to sleep. That would be self-defeating. Nor am I under-estimating the role execution plays in delivering the sales message of the commercial. After all, something has to call attention to the commercial in the first place, and that some-thing had better be an attention-riveting execution. I just want to restore that delicate balance which must exist be-tween concept and execution before a commercial can be called true advertising. And if, in the process of restoration, the execution returns to its proper place as the vehicle for putting across the selling idea clearly and believably, I'll consider my time to have been well spent.

The Great Show Biz Era—in which execution dominates concept, comedy writers replace copywriters, and film di-rectors supplant art directors—is personified by the recent 1930s spectacular for Great American soups, starring Ann Miller. I've heard some pretty far-out figures of what it cost to produce, ranging from $150,000 to $200,000, and I've also heard it costs $50,000 in residuals every time it runs. They've got to sell a helluva lot of soup to break even on this dribble, and I'm betting they won't make it.

If you can find one reason to buy the soup (instead of a Campbell's standard), one sales point, one functional reason for the thirties motif, one marketing concept, one logical reason for its existence as a piece of advertising, I'll buy a whole movie-theaterful of that soup.

It simply isn't enough justification to say that its objective was to build brand awareness in a market dominated by another brand. That's a cop-out excuse that could be used by any product in any category that isn't number one in its class. Moreover, it isn't what you'd call a specific objective, or even a worthwhile one when you think about it. People don't buy products simply because they know of their exis-tence. Building "brand awareness" is not enough; I expect a lot more from a commercial than that. It has to give me a reason to try the brand over the brand I'm now using.

And this commercial offers no such reason.

So it simply isn't advertising, and the person who could create a commercial like this one obviously knows a whole lot more about show biz than he does about advertising. To prove my point, the creator of this commercial proudly states that he had been nurturing this idea for four years, just waiting for a client who could "appreciate the value of a nostalgic trip to the thirties. . . ." (Another client had turned it down before because of its price tag).

Well, I've got news for him: Good commercials, concepts, and executions are *not* interchangeable. Each commercial has to be tailor-made for a particular product according to that product's particular marketing strategy. Does our Great American soup creator think that commercials should be generic with just the name of the product filled in? And what about the client who bought the idea? *He* should be smart enough to know about individualized commercials for individualized marketing strategies better than anyone else. But even if this client pleads innocence by virtue of advertising ignorance, how can he ever live with his conscience for having squandered that kind of money? What will he say to his stockholders?

If there's a bright side to inflation and the tight money situation, it must be that we're going to see fewer of these monsters in the future. We've already seen too many of them in the past.

Like the one thrust upon an unsuspecting public in behalf of Contac Cold Remedy. Called "Cold Diggers of 1969," it won every industry award you could name that year. I'm still at a loss to understand why, since it has to be the most overproduced commercial of all time. Starting with a good concept—*Take Good Care of Yourself, You Belong to Me*—it should have succeeded. For one thing, the line represents a shrewd thrust into the male market via an attempt to picture men as strong defenders who must "take good care" of themselves because their women depend upon them, a strategy that overcomes traditional male reluctance to pamper an ordinary cold with medication. This is a concept he can live with, because it allows him to obtain the relief he's been aching for and still hold on to his masculinity. Simultaneously, the concept appeals to the motherly instincts of its women viewers by presenting them with a moral obligation to guard their loved ones' health.

Now then. Here was a fine little idea which translated itself nicely into print. On TV, a first attempt came off rather well as spots showed loving women taking care of their equally loving men with Contac. No one who watched the commercials could fail to get the message.

Then this campaign caught cold and died. And out of the fevered imagination of a desperate agency came forth the Contac Cold Diggers of 1969.

Nothing less than full-cast musical comedy takeoffs on the gold digger films of the thirties, these commercials featured brigades of properly tweezed and frizzed chorus girls dancing and singing in the best Ziegfeld manner to the *Take Good Care of Yourself* theme, replete with neon rainbows and revolving Busby Berkeley sets.

And that was that.

No sales message, no pitch. No tie-in to the theme song like the one that worked so well for the first campaign. Just a minute or so of *Shuffle off to Buffalo* unrelieved by any clear, directional message. Thanks so much, Contac, for that amusing production number to break up the tedium of our nightly television fare. Next time you might slip in a word or two for your product, if you like, but don't feel obliged to if altruism suits you better.

That wasn't really the "Cold Diggers." It was "Death of a Sales Idea," a tragedy in 60 seconds. In case you think I'm being unduly severe, please realize that this sponsor paid thousands of dollars for the privilege of knowing that his commercial was being apostrophized, in living rooms across the land, as "cute." Not "compelling," mind you, but "cute."

If I were that sponsor, I'd damn well demand less cute entertainment and more sales talk for my advertising dollar. Nor would I spend one groat on a memorable line if the line didn't contain my product's name in it. Alka-Seltzer's didn't either, and they were rewarded with the great granddaddy of show biz commercials, the *Try It You'll Like It* series. Think of it! The two creative originators of this campaign were lionized as heros of the "new" Madison Avenue. Their famous line—and a second one, *I Can't Believe I Ate the Whole Thing*—slipped effortlessly into common parlance, a fact that caused the normally sober *New York Times* to gush that this was:

> . . . the most successful advertising campaign of last year, if public recognition is the criterion (85% of Americans questioned could identify Alka-Seltzer with the commercials); some say it is the most successful television campaign ever. The two favorite lines from the series . . . [I Can't Believe I Ate the Whole Thing and Try It, You'll Like It] . . . appear as slogans on sweatshirts, in supermarket windows, even on church marquees; they serve as the punch lines for innumerable and still proliferating jokes—many of them obscene—and at least one of the lines is likely to be repeated at most social gatherings anywhere in the United States.

And through it all, I stoutly maintained that I can't believe I *hate* the whole thing because this campaign wasn't advertising.

For openers, no matter what *The New York Times* thinks, recognition is *not* the criterion for advertising success when it comes to a product as well known and heavily advertised as Alka-Seltzer. Believability, conviction, persuasion, and, of course, conversion of non-users and users of competitive brands—these factors determine whether a well-known product's campaign is successful or not, and they add up to *sales*.

Secondly, although it's very nice for the copywriters that their lines were being repeated so enthusiastically, I'm not sure what advantage that gave to the client. Because this series was far better entertainment than advertising, the waggish punch lines are far better remembered than the reasons for buying the product. The "entertaining" commercial can be a well-financed ego trip for its creators.

Let's get back to the *Times* article for a moment. The article stated that the agency responsible for the Alka-Seltzer campaign modestly feared a backlash against "unfunny" commercials in the future. It goes on to confirm that the formula for creating these commercials was first to come up with a funny, memorable punch line and *then* to write a commercial around it. In short, suit the sales idea to the execution, instead of beginning the other way around. This may be the right way to sell funny lines to the buying public, but I can't believe it's the right way to go about selling a product.

Finally, the article quotes the president of the agency on the subject of the American consumer. Her observations are particularly ironic in light of the events that followed.

> The overindulgent American is an average consumer. We understand him . . . because we're average consumers ourselves. We're *now* people. We use Alka-Seltzer, we talk like people in the commercials, we can identify with smiley situations. I'm

fascinated with the American consumer today. He's just so smart.

And those may be the funniest lines of all.

Because agency people just aren't average consumers. They are, as she noted, "now people," marketing oriented and far too hip to have much in common with average anybodies. She was right about one thing, though. American consumers *are* smart. So smart that they quoted the punch lines and didn't buy the campaign. Or the product. Shortly thereafter, the smiley situations were replaced by real commercials that sold Alka-Seltzer instead of *bon mots*. And suddenly, I loved the whole thing.

They got rid of the show biz. The entertainment. The jokes, the punch lines, the actors, and the elaborate productions. In their place, they introduced some of the simplest commercials I've ever seen, and some of the best. Each one consisted of a close-up of an on-camera spokesman—not a famous personality, but a plain, believable, next-door-neighborly human being—who delivers the entire message face-to-face, person-to-person, with no frills and no bull. His message is straightforward and honest, stressing how effective Alka-Seltzer can be in combating upset stomachs and headaches. He offers us solid reasons why we should use Alka-Seltzer instead of a competing brand: first, for its specially buffered aspirin and antacids, second, because it's the best remedy you can buy without a prescription. If it doesn't work, you'd better see your doctor. (A strong statement like that instills confidence in the product.) Third, you should buy Alka-Seltzer because it's a potent medicine, not a candy-store patent remedy. (A repositioning statement that treats the product with the seriousness it deserves as a cure for a serious problem. After all, what's funny about an upset stomach?) Finally, the commercial establishes the efficacy of the product by warning us not to take it every time some little thing bothers us, but, like any medicine, to save it for when we really need it. They even took advantage of Alka-Seltzer's long history on the American scene by promoting their history in commercials aimed at the older market. It's been around for a long while, these commercials say, and we have faith in it.

The concept and positioning of that new campaign was absolutely right. The execution was brilliantly simple, completely believable, highly persuasive, and totally honest. It made the old show biz Alka-Seltzer spots look a little distasteful, a little silly, a little contrived, a little inappropriate, a little incompatible with the nature of the product—and then suddenly, the whole dumb series seemed about as appetizing and as convincing as a big spicy meat-a-ball. If I'm wrong and this straight-from-the-shoulder campaign didn't do a better job of selling Alka-Seltzer than the ethnic situation comedies, then I'm ready to get the hell out of the business.

And as a reward, if I'm right, I'll settle for the difference in production costs between the old campaign and the new one.

I have a lot of respect for Alka-Seltzer for diagnosing and correcting their own mistake. The unfunny sales results produced by their funny campaign prove that cause and effect is truly a factor in advertising, and the buying public has a say in the kind of advertising we see on our TV screens. It also proves that jokes, entertainment, and big-budget commercials don't sell the product if the sales idea isn't there to begin with.

Many advertisers who were captivated by the idea of "humorous" commercials took an object lesson from the Alka-Seltzer case. A few didn't, and they failed. One—Dr.

Pepper, to be exact—did a schizoid about-face with its humorous commercials that produced two distinct campaigns, with both plying the airwaves at the same time. So different were the results that it was hard to believe that a single agency produced both campaigns, that they both advertised the same product. One campaign proves my point—that jokes can't substitute for a selling idea—while the other shows how a humorous execution can be used well to complement a sound selling concept. Remember these?

Campaign #1

"With a name like Dr. Pepper it isn't easy to get people to try us. We're America's most misunderstood soft drink. You've got to try it to love it." These lines were the theme of the series. What do they mean, anyway? All they do is create a problem instead of offering us a solution; they never do get around to offering us a reason for trying the soft drink. Wouldn't it have been better to give us a hint about the *taste* of the new soft drink? It isn't even a very original theme; consider "With a name like Goodman's . . ." and "With a name like Smucker's . . ." to name just a couple.

Then those second two lines bother me. Just *what* misunderstanding are they talking about? Either convince me that there is, in fact, a misunderstanding, or clear it up for me, but don't just leave me hanging. And haven't I heard the last line somewhere? ("Trying is believing . . ." "You've got to taste it to believe it . . ." "Try it, you'll like it.")

But the theme lines are the least of these commercials' problems. Their executions are among the most puerile, nonsensical "comedy" sketches ever perpetrated upon a confused public, and none of them deserves the name "advertising." Take the Italian mother pleading with her bachelor son at the kitchen table, for example. "Anthony," she begs, "you're 42 years old. When are you going to try it?" From the folds of her motherly apron, she produces a Dr. Pepper, which he drinks to the triumphal strains of an overloud theme song. An announcer muddles the issue even further with the voiced-over sign-off, "With a name like Dr. Pepper, it isn't easy to get people to try us. . . ."

Or how about the two desperados trapped in the desert by a sadistic red-necked sheriff who gloatingly demands their surrender. To the escaped convicts, the choice between the sheriff and the vultures overhead is a tough one, but at last they give up for a bottle of Dr. Pepper. The theme song blares in the desert and the familiar voice-over delivers the familiar sign-off.

Then there are the astronauts, confronted by menacing Martians, who break out bottles of Dr. Pepper as peace offerings . . . and you know the rest.

Quite honestly, I don't know what these commercials are driving at. No one is *forcing* the public to try the soft drink, so why a whole campaign built around people being forced to try Dr. Pepper? These may be America's most misunderstood commercials. That's show biz!

Campaign #2

Now figure this out: here is the same product, with the same objective of selling to an audience of first-time triers. But this time the concept is a clear, simple bit of logic that we can deal with: "You've got to be good to make it in New York, and Dr. Pepper is making it." Maybe it's not the world's greatest line, but it tells me plenty and gives me a reason to try it. If everybody likes Dr. Pepper and it's catching on, it must be good, right?

And what a difference in execution! Here too, humor is used to get the theme across, but these commercials use realistic humor rather than contrived comedy. The difference between the two is the difference between advertising and show business.

Take the commercial that features a sidewalk pushcart hot dog hawker. Indigenous only to New York, he takes time out to talk to us while his impressed customer waits in the background slowly munching on a hot dog. The vendor complains that nobody used to talk to him. His customers used to ask for a hot dog and soda, hot dog and soda, and that's all. Nobody talked to him. Then he started selling Dr. Pepper and his customers began to ply him with questions about it. And now that Dr. Pepper is so popular, he's right back to where he started. Nobody talks to him. People just ask for hot dog and soda, only this time the soda is Dr. Pepper. Announcer voice-over glides in as the vendor turns resignedly back to his customer, noting that "You've got to be good to make it in New York, and Dr. Pepper is making it." Academy award material it isn't, but it's natural humor that comes from focusing on natural New Yorkers telling of their first experience with Dr. Pepper.

There's another memorable spot (among many) that concentrates on a black teenager, relaxing against a fence as a noisy schoolyard basketball game goes on behind him. In typical kid fashion, one of the onlookers keeps popping his head into the picture as all kids do when there's a camera around—a great, realistic touch. In a calm, straightforward way this teenager tells us that when he first heard of Dr. Pepper, he thought it was "medicine, man . . ." but after trying it, he thinks it's great. The omnipresent voice-over draws the right conclusion, and we go on about our daily business, convinced that Dr. Pepper is getting somewhere in New York because it's great.

As in all these commercials, the casting and photography are superb, amazingly realistic, and unbelievably believable. I swallowed every word these two told me because they were nonprofessional, un-slick, and true to life. I might meet either of them around any New York streetcorner tomorrow. The people, the dialect, and the locations are 100 percent New York—another big believability factor. And *this* campaign is simple enough and convincing enough to have been converted easily to radio. It sounds just as good without the video, proving that a great campaign is easily adaptable to all media. Campaign #1 could never survive without its sight-gag crutches.

As they say, you've got to be good to make it in New York. And these commercials are good enough to make Dr. Pepper acceptable in the Big Apple. All it takes is a sane proportion of idea to medium.

Do I believe in humorous approaches to advertising? Of course I do! But I also believe that an ad maker owes it to his client to ask himself these three questions before he communicates his sales message with a funny or "clever" execution:

1. Is it compatible with the nature of the product being sold? If his client is the local funeral home, he'd better think it through again.

2. Is it likely to detract from the seriousness, believability, or sincerity of the message? Again, an upset stomach is no laughing matter. When humor minimizes the importance of the malady, it also minimizes the importance of the cure.

3. Does it overpower or slow down the communication of the message? If it does, you're selling humor, not your product or service.

WHILE I'm on the topic of slowing down the communication of the message, I'd like to sing out about jingles, one of the most used and abused devices of both radio and television.

Generally, I don't believe in jingles as effective selling devices. By themselves, they're not advertising. The best and most believable advertising is what comes closest to duplicating the one-on-one encounter of a salesman and a prospect. If you were a salesman, would you sing your message?

People may wind up singing the words of your jingle without ever understanding or thinking about their meaning. (Take "The Star Spangled Banner," for example.) They remember the jingle, but not the message.

I think jingles can be used effectively to do two things, provided they are used with reasonable frequency. As an audio tag they can help register a product name (the famous *J-E-L-L-O* tag that made Jack Benny famous; Kellogg's *K-E-double-L-O-double-good, Kellogg's best to you* at the end of every cereal commercial; *N-E-S-T-L-E-S, Nestlés makes the very best, chocolate; That's what Campbell's soups are, m'mm m'mm good;* the Jolly Green Giant jingle), and they can act as a reminder of an already well-established fact or concept. The original "Pepsi-Cola hits the spot, 12 full ounces that's a lot" jingle launched a new soft drink by these reminders on radio (before the age of television, of course) of a heavy campaign in newspapers and magazines. Together they established the basic selling concept that Pepsi was twice as big as Coca-Cola for the same money; McDonald's *You deserve a break today* theme; *Have it your way* from Burger King; *When you say Bud, you've said it all;* Coke's *"It's the real thing;* Tetley's *Tiny little tea leaves* jingle.

Jingles should never be relied upon to carry, deliver, or establish a basic selling message.

However, I do admit, they're great for the shower.

THE only reason for the existence of any commercial is to communicate an idea from the advertiser to the viewer. It is not a vehicle for entertainment. If it leaves you howling with glee, or whistling a tune, the chances are good that it didn't simultaneously leave you making plans for the purchase of its product. You simply haven't got time to concentrate on both. As an advertiser, I'd much rather let you arrange for your own entertainment through movies, plays, books, sex. Show biz isn't the advertising business, and the two make strange bedfellows on the TV screen. This is not to say that commercials cannot or should not be entertaining. So long as the entertainment is functional in communicating the idea, I'm all in favor of it. But I get mad as hell when I see Hollywood people, sets, and budgets taking over my business.

The kind of people who belong in the advertising business are ad people with bright new ideas about how to *reach* and *convince* other people in 60 seconds or less. That's damned hard to do. Which is why these people, the real innovators and professionals, should stay in complete control of a commercial from start to finish. The alternative is for them to surrender their brainchild, the single most precious product of our business, to the swash and swagger of a loud, wasteful, and unnecessary swarm of technical parasites. And that would be untenable. It would be suicidal. It would be cowardly.

And it wouldn't be advertising.

6
Irrelevance vs. Simplicity

Just to prove that the shortest distance between two points is a straight line, look at the following examples of recent TV commercials that don't waste time or cloud the issue when it comes to transmitting the sales message from advertiser to audience. Then look at the ones that both waste *and* cloud, asking yourself if their creators were merely clumsy—or desperate to hide the fact that they had no sales story.

Take Gablinger's beer. As the first beer to be introduced with a really exciting, tangible product difference in a long, long time, Gablinger's was an advertiser's dream. Imagine! The first beer without carbohydrates! The sales message *is* the product!

In print (magazines and newspapers, that is) the advertiser took direct aim at the audience and fired the sales message in a single, clean, straight line: "Gablinger's: the first beer without carbohydrates." Bingo! Anything else they could have said about the product at this point would have been superfluous.

Then the advertiser turned his attention to TV and an interesting situation developed.

The first TV commercial showed us Gablinger's Unique Advantage as simply as possible by stressing the point that every time you drink a glass of beer you're taking in the carbohydrate equivalent of a whole slice of white bread—without the nutritional value. Two glasses, and you've gobbled down two slices. Three glasses, three slices. Then it introduced Gablinger's as the first and only beer with no carbohydrates at all. Visually the demonstration is great: A slushy, soggy piece of bread floats in a mug of beer to remind us that ordinary beer is filling and heavy. Stare at that glutinous blob long enough and you begin to imagine how it must look in your stomach. If you're not ready for a diet beer then, you're a hopeless endomorph.

The slogan is emphatic—"Won't fill you up!"—and it tells the heavy beer drinkers at whom the commercial is aimed that they can drink several beers at one sitting without the carbohydrate menace of poor health and beer bellies. The commercial makes its single, strong point as simply as possible. Dramatic and believable in its presentation, this commercial sold me on the product's advertising agency as well as the product itself. Until I saw the second commercial, that is.

A beer drinking contest takes place in a small pool room behind a saloon. The two opponents are being cheered on by kibbitzers whose sensitive palates were obviously ripened at Attica State Prison. Our contestants match glass for glass until the larger and cruder of the two discovers that the other guy has been drinking Gablinger's all along. That's unfair, of course, because everybody knows Gablinger's doesn't fill you up. Well, this is a roundabout way of saying so, but up to this point, I'll buy it. The point was made, albeit badly, and the commercial should have stopped there.

It didn't.

Instead, the big guy propels the little guy through the door and dumps him on his fanny on the barroom floor. What sales point, please, does *that* illustrate? I get a cheap, old-fashioned low-status feeling about the beer from this commercial, just the opposite, I'm sure, of what Gablinger's wants me to feel about the product. The brawl just plain took over and so diminished the subject of the commercial that it *became* the commercial. It should have landed on the editing room floor along with the beaten contestant.

Why didn't it?

This is only a theory, mind you, but it's historically demonstrable that Gablinger's bombed the first time around because all those first-time triers who rushed to taste the only no-carbohydrate beer never came back for a second taste. Obviously, the introductory commercial was *too* good because it got too many people to try a beer they would never buy a second time. Therefore, the only solution must have been to try to sell less beer.

I'm kidding, of course, but maybe that's why the commercials that told the carbohydrate story so simply, so beautifully, so believably, gave way to a lot of irrelevancies. They certainly couldn't move on to talk about taste, could they? Nor could they point to Gablinger's as the favorite of thousands when plainly it was not. Even their hold upon the dieters was a tenuous one, because like everyone else, dieters have a limit on how much they are willing to sacrifice for vanity. The only answer was to create terrible commercials. And that's what they did so well.

After that, everything degenerated into irrelevance. One of the clearest examples I can remember was a spot that opened in what appeared to be a smoker or a stag testimonial dinner. It was attended by a dozen tuxedo-clad men sitting around a conference table in a smoke-filled room. Each, in turn, gets up to praise Dr. Hersch Gablinger. One even toasts the forgotten little woman. One man pays tribute to the boys in the yeast room, and another inebriated valedictorian salutes the bowling team. The entire mood of the commercial, from the casting to the dress, the lighting, and the camera angles, was carefully calculated to evoke the prohibition era. How cute. What it failed to evoke, however, was a single good reason why you or I should sprint to the store to buy a six-pack of Gablinger's.

I just have to believe that a sales point the sponsor himself believes in should come wrapped in a commercial without a trace of fat on it. When they introduce *anything* that does not in some way contribute to that message—an extra line, a prop that doesn't belong there, or a whole sequence that rounds out the commercial itself instead of the product message—I start asking myself why they're distracting my attention from the product. Because the product does not perform is the obvious answer. Such was the case with Gablinger's beer, but that's no excuse for poor advertising.

Next in line for the smokescreen award comes Bayer for the entire campaign they built around the "fact" that many truisms aren't really true. In one commercial, a man dressed à la 1492 asserts that the world is definitely flat. Cut (where a scene ends abruptly and another scene begins, in contrast to a dissolve where one scene fades gradually into the next) to a primitive-looking plane crashing on takeoff. "If man were meant to fly," states a smug onlooker, "he'd have wings." Cut to a woman emphatically claiming that all aspirin is the same. Suddenly an announcer breaks in to point out that truisms are not always true. All aspirin, for instance, is *not* the same, because Bayer, tested against all aspirin, tested better.

What a logistic house of cards *that* is! Even the very best analogies are usually wasteful and unnecessary. These weren't even analogous to the product being sold, but rather to some silly point of reference that has nothing to do with aspirin. When you consider that better than 50 percent of the commercial's time and about 95 percent of its production budget were wasted on the elaborate analogies rather than spent to tell the sales story, you begin to wonder where the sponsor was when the agency delivered the storyboard. If the tests really *were* conclusive, why didn't they devote all their time and money to telling us about the results? The fact that they chose not to do so makes me somewhat wary of those "results." Again, I get the feeling that I'm being fast-talked. Not clearly, of course, and not simply. Just very, very fast.

With a backward nod to the preceding chapter, I'd like to say that believability was irreparably damaged by those silly little sketches, which were not only irrelevant, but totally incompatible with the serious nature of the product and its message. Nobody takes aspirin for fun; it's just not a "fun" product. I have to assume that the tests conducted were not funny, either, nor were their results. So why use humor when the objective was to convince people that this aspirin is different from the others? Humor is a headache here.

In contrast, Bufferin released a commercial at approximately the same time that focused squarely on the product. It was a simple commercial with nothing irrelevant added. I have no reason to suspect that this commercial isn't telling me the truth.

A suffering man lies in bed, stricken with the miseries of the flu or a cold. Then, thermometer markings appear, superimposed over him as he lies in bed. His temperature starts to climb and so does the mercury in the thermometer. The announcer says, "Turn down the heat with Bufferin," and we watch as the man takes Bufferin and his temperature gradually falls. The announcer then explains why Bufferin brings down fever from colds and flu better than aspirin. What could be more simple, more graphic, or more convincing? They knew what they wanted to say, so they said it quickly, honestly, and believably, without a lot of doubletalk or shaky logic to muddy the issue.

It's foolish to try to dope out some ulterior meaning in every commercial that depends upon irrelevancies for its punch, because a lot of such nonsense is the result of stupidity, not cupidity. Take Korvettes' campaign not so long ago, in which the "Mayor of Korvette" (a Fiorello La Guardia look-alike wearing a fireman's hat) toots a horn and bangs away on a set of drums every time a Korvettes sale is made. Quite aside from the fact that it draws a rather unkind caricature of one of New York's best-loved mayors, this commercial's undoing is the introduction of the mayor at all. Why in the world does Korvettes need a mayor? And what, pray, does he do for the consumer? Certainly Korvettes didn't need to elect its own mayor just to illustrate a new slogan, "Us little guys fight back"—that slogan has been used successfully for some time by a local supermarket chain *without* a mayor. Is someone here trying to associate Korvettes with the former mayor of New York? Or to identify the company as a "little guy"? They could have used a jockey, or even a midget. But why? And why Fiorello? Far better would have been some hard facts about Korvettes' merchandise or service, presented simply and straightforwardly. The point about the mayor was difficult to understand, and once understood (but not by me), utterly irrelevant. And how much sympathy can Korvettes hope to gain with this "little guy" slogan when they are themselves a retail giant?

And then there was the ultimate irrelevance in the Honda commercial, where a spokesman, walking around a Honda car, compares it feature by feature with an apple—yes, an apple—perched upon a stool nearby. "This Honda seats four comfortably. This apple holds two, maybe three, worms—tops." At the end of the commercial, the announcer eats the apple, grimaces, and stalks off. He might as well have eaten the car for all the sense it made. I won't even bother to point out why this spot doesn't work; I have too much respect for your judgment. Let me just ask instead: When was the last time you bought a car because it was roomier than an apple?

Honda must share the prize for the ultimate irrelevance with another campaign which, strangely enough, also compares its product to a fruit: the Bic Banana. Despite all the money the manufacturer spent to develop and promote the Banana (a name I'll never understand), I talk to people from time to time who still don't know that the Banana is a felt-tip pen, a tiny news item the commercial should be taking care of because Bic is a name that's synonymous with ball-point pens. Now I would think that it must be explained clearly, definitely, simply, and unmistakably that the Bic Banana is *not* a ball-point pen but a felt-tip marker. *That's* what their ads should be aiming for. Instead, we're treated to a singing classroom, cavemen, Shakespeare, and who-knows-what in the future so that the sponsor can make the association between his product and . . . er . . . a banana. It's so embarrassing, it's painful to say. A banana. You know, a banana doesn't even write.

I take it all back about the tied winners for the ultimate irrelevance award. Bic wins it peels down.

Irrelevant material, then, that distracts us from the sales message, is trying to tell us something. It's either trying to say that there *is* no sales message (or, possibly, that the product's advertising agency has failed to discern it properly) or that the agency has hired a film crew instead of advertising people to do the commercial. The commercials cited as examples were not about the product. They were about apples and bananas or dancing soup cans or maybe even the director's poor little libido laminated between strips of celluloid for all the world to see. Don't let them fool you.

This is what you should be watching: One black man stands on one white beach. He tells us that it costs about $50 a day to enjoy yourself in the Caribbean, and for that kind of money you deserve to know what kind of weather you're going to get. The three Virgin Islands (St. Croix, St. Thomas, and St. John) have the best weather in all the Caribbean. A string of $50 perfect, sunny days, practically guaranteed.

Mind you, all this information is presented by a single man on a single beach. No props. No gimmicks. No dancing natives or scenes of night life, no moonstruck lovers, postcard sunsets, bikinis, or tables groaning with ersatz French cuisine. Just straight honest talk about a subject (weather) that's bound to interest anyone who's been thinking of taking a trip to a warmer climate.

Commercials like this renew my faith in the power of simple advertising and confirm the weakness of extravagant productions. They reinforce my conviction that the simpler the commercial is, the greater the believability. Stated another way, believability seems to rise or fall in inverse proportion to the cost of the production. That's a little theorem my cohorts have begun to call "Seiden's Law." It holds true, whether you're talking about the Virgin Islands or . . .

Midas mufflers. Remember the campaign that established Midas as the muffler specialists by cutting out the competition they were getting from gas stations? The campaign accomplished it very simply. One commercial showed us a crew of gas station workers trying to figure out how to install a muffler. Another showed us a gas station manager having a car lowered from the lift when its owner inquires about his muffler guarantee ("Take it up, Voigil. Take it down, Voigil.").

This was a strong, memorably executed campaign. It established the fact that because Midas does mufflers and only mufflers, Midas does it quicker, better, and more economically than any gas station can do it. And they guarantee their work for the life of the car.

I don't know how anyone who has seen these commercials could ever again go to his gas station to have a muffler installed. It would be like going to your friendly G.P. for open-heart surgery. This campaign has the Midas touch.

You kind of get the same feeling from the commercial that introduced Arm & Hammer laundry detergent. After watching this one, you'd feel like a criminal buying an old pollutant for washing your clothes. Not because the commercial makes you feel guilty, mind you, but just because it presents the product's advantages so forcefully and simply. It pictures (and talks about) the natural beauty of our lakes and streams and explains how detergents pollute them. Then, unceremoniously and totally without pretention, it introduces the new nonpolluting Arm & Hammer detergent. No drums, no bugles, no white tornados, no galloping knight. Just a beautifully simple, sincere, and powerful sales message compatible with the product.

It certainly makes the rest of the fanfare and fol-de-rol look foolish, doesn't it? And it tells me that the sponsor is proud enough of his product to want to present it on an unobtrusive velvet cushion that sets off the product's advantages to perfection. That's what a commercial is meant to do in the first place: highlight the product's advantages. All the hoopla is only an absurd distraction in an attempt to cover for the lack of an advantage. It never fools anyone.

Now that you know enough to tell the one from the other, can you ever again watch a muddled commercial through the same innocent eyes?

7
The Pure and Simple School of Advertising

FOR MY MONEY, THE ONLY SCHOOL OF ADVERTISING WORTH the price of tuition is the "Pure and Simple" school. Admittedly, it's not very fashionable. It's not terribly chic to admit you're a graduate. Its alumni aren't famous enough to be invited to the better industry social gatherings or award dinners. But I'm a believer and I just couldn't feel at home in the fancier, snobbier, more sophisticated schools. They're not my style. And I suspect they're not even very good.

The essential lesson taught by the "Pure and Simple" school is that advertising must have something to say. Beyond that, what it has to say is all-important. Finally, advertising should say it straight, plain and simple. It's a straightforward credo, and one that's particularly applicable to the medium of television where so many temptations are available to distract from the message.

I love to see one simple objective for a campaign established, and I like to see it tackled head-on. I have no patience for subtlety, finesse, deviousness, velvet gloves, and syrupy tongues. I hate hidden meanings. (I never understand them anyway. In movies or plays or books, my wife has to explain all the hidden meanings to me later.) Like most people, I take everything at face value because I don't like to spend time and effort figuring out what somebody *really* meant. Why not just *say* it? Life is too short and time too precious—especially TV time—for advertisers to beat around the bush.

So I'm generally against any kind of advertising that relegates the product to a secondary position or treats it as anything less than the hero of the commercial. Oh, I suppose that even a "Pure and Simple" graduate can admit that there are times when the most direct route between product and prospect may not be a straight line. For those cases I offer only two cautions: you better have a damn good reason for it, and it better be good.

Shell gasoline used this strategy recently in its "If Shell can make this, you know they make good gasoline" campaign, and it worked. (This, of course, was prior to the gasoline shortage.) After all, what can you say about gasoline that hasn't already been said, one way or another, a dozen times before? If Shell didn't sell its product directly in this campaign, it's probably because consumers regard gasoline as a parity product that offers slight (if any) difference between brands.

As a matter of fact, the statistics are on their side. Research shows that people won't even cross the street for a particular brand, because the single most important factor in picking one brand of gas over another is the convenience of the service station. That's why premiums and games and stamps have always played such a large role in gasoline marketing. Without a real difference in the product to hang their advertising on, gas dealers have had to manufacture a difference in service or to advertise by association, as Shell did in this campaign.

By associating Shell gas with the expertise, research, and scope of its parent company, the three commercials I saw in this campaign did a fine selling job with a product that simply can't be sold on its own merits. In one commercial, a spokesman demonstrated the "Pancake," an ingeniously simple, tarlike self-lubricant for railroad cars. Another showed an oil slick spreading on a body of water. A new product from Shell research is squirted around the slick by men circling the slick in rowboats. As we watch, the slick condenses to the size of a basketball and is easily removed from the water. A third commercial dealt with slip-proof boating sneakers that were praised by a sailing enthusiast and demonstrated by his crew. The point of all the commercials, of course, was the theme line: "If Shell can make this, you know they make good gasoline, because that's their main business." I think Shell was very shrewd in the choice of this "excellence by association" technique. I like the campaign in spite of the fact that I usually hate borrowed interest. In this product category, I think it's justifiable, and although the execution was by no means creatively inspired, it seemed to work.

Just as often, though, advertisers who make an indirect pitch fall on their faces. They would have done much better with a pure and simple demonstration of the differences between their product and someone else's.

Take Datsun's "Drive a Datsun, plant a tree" campaign, for instance, which promised to plant a tree in a U.S. forest if you'd come in and test-drive a Datsun. I saw two of them, one with Steve Allen as the spokesman and another narrated by a famous conservationist whose name meant nothing to me. This campaign really advertised a promotion, not a car, and that bothered me. But that's not what bothered me most. In fact, I think it may be a good idea for an off-brand like Datsun to use promotions to build traffic and encourage trial, as long as the product itself doesn't get lost along the way.

My major problem with the Datsun campaign stems from the fact that its promotion gimmick is incompatible with its product. What do trees have to do with cars? Couldn't they have come up with a better promotion for something as tangible as a car? Tree planting might be a good theme for a newspaper or a greeting card company, a furniture manufacturer or a wood paneling supplier. All of these products are nearly 100 percent dependent upon trees as a source for their raw material, and forest depletion is their biggest nightmare. But forcing a connection between *cars* and trees is the ultimate nonsequitur. How much better it would have been if the Datsun people had given you a good reason for wanting to test-drive their car! Trees may be an extra-added-attraction, but they're not in themselves a reason for buying this car rather than another car. An automobile is one of the most considered purchases we make (probably second only to buying a house), and nobody buys or tries one because they're feeling philanthropic that day. Even a "Pure and Simple" sophomore would have suggested a few sales points in an attempt to interest the audience in the *car* rather than the promotion. In this case, we don't see the product for the trees.

(I have one more problem with the promotion, and it's purely a personal one: I always suspect the motives behind charitable acts performed for commercial gain. If Datsun is so concerned with conservation, why don't they just go ahead and plant the trees anyway? Why must it be conditional to trying their car? I guess I expect people to be charitably motivated from the bottom of their hearts, rather than from the depth of their pocketbooks. I resent philanthropies with strings attached and so does the rest of the American public. To offer a starving man your food is humanitarianism at its best. But to put your name on it is commercialism at its worst. The United States has been criticized for doing just that ever since we became the world's largest philanthropic organization. This time the name is made in Japan.)

Given my attitude toward indirect advertising, you can imagine how excited I got when I saw a new campaign break on TV not so long ago that graduated *summa cum laude* from the "Pure and Simple" school. It has a well-defined, simple objective delivered in a straight-from-the-gut manner. It didn't feature award-winning copy or graphics, and it'll never win an advertising award, but it *did* win my heart and my fervent admiration for its simple approach to the truth. For a change, a commercial isn't trying to snow me. If this campaign doesn't accomplish its objective then I'm ready to give up the advertising business and take up something more solid and professional. Like race-track touting.

I'm talking about the campaign for B. F. Goodrich tires. You know the one—it clears up the confusion that exists because the names "Goodrich" and "Goodyear" sound so much alike. For years that confusion has plagued the Goodrich people, and this campaign represents their first attempt to tackle the problem head on.

The commercials in this campaign are honest about their objective, even going so far as to state that the confusion has always worked to the advantage of their competitor because Goodyear is by far the larger of the two companies in tire manufacturing. It has more retail outlets, does considerably more advertising, and is generally better known by the public. So Goodrich has had to cope with a vicious circle: the more money they spent on advertising their product, the more they were selling their competitor's product. Finally, they did what had to be done to clear up the confusion decisively, quickly, and unmistakably with this bite-the-bullet campaign.

But that's not all that happens in these commercials. They also manage to set the Goodrich name apart from Goodyear by informing the public that it was Goodrich who first introduced the revolutionary steel-belted radial tires to this country, and that's all they've advertised for the last five years. (Goodyear, on the other hand, is still primarily advertising conventional tires.) So cleverly conceived is their campaign to set themselves apart from Goodyear that they even use Goodyear's most famous symbol, the Goodyear blimp, to their own advantage. "We're the ones without the blimp," notes one Goodrich commercial. I think that's beautiful!

There were two original commercials that launched this campaign. One featured the president of the company and the other centered on a Goodrich dealer. The campaign continued with two delightful executions of the same theme that followed. One featured a precocious red-headed boy of about eight or nine sitting on the desk of his Goodrich-dealer dad. He proudly informs his father that when he grows up he intends to follow in his father's footsteps and become a Goodrich dealer. He asks his dad if then he'll be able to take a ride in the blimp. When his father breaks it to him that Goodrich doesn't have a blimp, it belongs to those other guys, the boy hesitates a moment and then disappointedly announces that he thinks he'll become a lawyer instead.

The next entry in the campaign featured an Italian mother who pleads with her Goodrich-dealer son for a ride in the blimp. She is equally disappointed to learn that they don't have one.

These were two more superb executions in a continuing superb campaign that is wearing well over the years. Obviously it's making an impact. Early in 1976 Goodrich announced that this "We're the other guys" campaign (also known as the non-blimp campaign) proved to be "one of the most successful ever created in the tire industry." In only three years since the birth of the campaign, Goodrich brand awareness increased 122 percent. What's more, preference for BFG radials rose a whopping 85 percent, while tire sales and market penetration climbed. That, after a lifetime of confusion and playing second fiddle to Goodyear. (So I guess my career as a race-track tout will have to wait.)

It's always gratifying to discover that good advertising can be both creative *and* effective. And beyond that, the Goodrich campaign strikes a blow for the "Pure and Simple" school of advertising. It made me think, for the first time in many years, of an old client who once summed up his philosophy of advertising to his agency with this crude little ditty: "Tell me quick and tell me true, or else my dear the hell with you." The same client used to hurl another bit of doggerel at the agency creative people that went something like: "If you can't make it great, play it straight." They took his advice on both counts. As I recall, they never won any awards for the advertising they did on this account, but oh boy did they build a business!

Tell it pure and tell it simple, Goodrich. Your alma mater is proud of you.

8
Print:
The Mother Medium

JUST BECAUSE MOST OF THE CHAPTERS IN THIS BOOK CON-
centrate on television, don't get the idea that this is a book
about television advertising.

It's not.

Because everything I've got to say about good advertising
pertains to all media. I've merely used TV commercials
rather than print ads as examples throughout this book because television is the single most dramatic, effective, and
dominant medium for mass communication in the world
today. More national advertising dollars are being poured
into it than into all other media combined. And it's going to
become even more dominant in the future. You can bet on it.

But print isn't dead yet. It's just changed from what it
was a short generation ago.

Print began changing when it became *a* medium instead
of *the* medium. Now I'm no media expert. A real one could
tick off the reasons for the change in the print medium much

more authoritatively than I can. And he or she could give you a broader overview of the consequences of this change, too.

I am giving you, however, my personal viewpoint of what really happened as I saw it, and I had a pretty good view as promotion manager of a major magazine at the time. In those days, print was not just *the* medium, it was *my* medium, so I can talk about the collapse of magazines from firsthand experience. I was there. I was one of the first casualties. I lost my job.

Close your eyes for a moment and imagine yourself back in the 1950s. Magazines were the glamour girls of the media parade, remember? You subscribed to quite a few. We all did. They were beautiful, they were entertaining. They were an unhurried pleasure on a winter's night, a faithful companion of the lonely, the curious, the shut-in. Everybody loved magazines. But no one more than the advertising people who prepared ads for them.

There was nothing more exciting for an art director or copywriter than creating a full-page, full-color ad for a big, prestigious mass magazine. You remember them—*Life, Look, Saturday Evening Post,* and *Colliers,* known as the Big Four to folks on the inside. Only slightly less prestigious were those two giants of the Sunday supplement field: *This Week* and *The American Weekly.* To see your work in any of these publications was to feel that, at long last, you had arrived. Who would have dreamed that within the space of a few short years these institutions (to say nothing of *Liberty, American,* and *Woman's Home Companion*) would be gone. They live only in nostalgic tales of the Good Old Days told by middle-aged men to their disinterested, unimpressed children with eyes glued to the TV and ears plastered against transistor radios. Must we really ask "What happened?"

Television happened! And magazines would never be the same again.

Pig-headedly, they mobilized to fight this new medium which had dared to challenge them—not collectively, of course, but individually. Instead of learning to live with TV (and, by extension, learning to share advertising dollars with it), magazines got greedy and attacked television. They used cost-per-reader versus cost-per-viewer comparisons. They invoked the added value of a lasting printed impression to ridicule the TV image as a fleeting moment in time. Sumptuous print reproductions, especially of food, were pitted against the inferior pictures on the TV screen. Editors flaunted their magazines' superior editorial environment for selling products. Magazines published audience demographic comparisons in an attempt to denigrate the quality of the TV viewer. Starch numbers (results compiled by the Daniel E. Starch Company, an independent research firm, which audits magazine advertising readership ad by ad) were sent to advertisers. They even offered reduced combination rates for advertisers who ran an ad in more than one of a publisher's magazines, though this turned out to be more a battle among publishers scrambling for their dwindling share of advertising dollars than an assault on television.

Before they were through, magazines had used every weapon they could get their hands on to force the impudent young upstart, television, to back down. They attacked television head on, and they got their heads handed to them.

Nothing worked because efficiency, numbers, reproduction, impressions, and editorial content were not the issues. The real issue was that a revolutionary change in America's life style had taken place that magazines refused to recognize. This change brought excitement and entertainment into the homes of Americans who never had much of either.

How many people are going to pay to read a book when they can see the movie free? It soon became clear that television could beat magazines at their own numbers games as more and more sets found their way into living rooms across the country. Magazines could never again compete with television for the mass, general audience. But magazines blindly plunged ahead in a battle they couldn't win. And the Big Four became three . . . then two . . . then one . . . and then there were none.

In retrospect, it's easy to say that magazines did all the wrong things to halt the TV juggernaut. Nothing could have stopped TV, really, but I still feel that something could have been done to save magazines. What would have happened if magazines had stopped fighting among themselves and had gotten together with combination rates that offered advertisers their choice of *any* magazines, regardless of publisher? They might even have added newspapers to the combination rate in an all-out effort to save the entire print industry. TV was hurting newspapers, too (of which, more anon).

And what if magazines had even made a deal with the TV networks themselves? Surely they could have hammered out combination rates promoting the use of TV and magazines together as the perfect media mix, either nationally or in specific markets. That would have been the wisest solution of all, because magazines and television complement each other in saturating a market.

No doubt about it. Many of the magazines that folded could have learned to live happily ever after with TV had they been willing to change. After decades of wrestling with the demon television, magazines are now cohabiting with TV by selling themselves on their own exclusive advantage over television. How? They're selling class instead of mass. Special interest instead of general interest. The war is over.

At least I thought so. As of this writing, over 20 years after the big magazine-TV war, the following ad, one in a campaign, is running for *Newsweek* in the trade press:

MIGHTIER THAN MAUDE:

(illustration: the covers of *Newsweek* and *Time*)
When *Newsweek* plus *Time* can deliver a larger audience than Maude can, it's time to rethink television.

What can be mightier than Maude? It's not Phyllis. Or the Six Million Dollar Man. It's not even a TV show. It's *Newsweek* plus *Time*—one of the strongest media buys you can make today: efficient, effective, and highly selective. Ask your media planning experts. *Newsweek*, to start with, reaches an audience of 19 million adults—a rating of 13.6. And that's just *Newsweek*. Add *Time* and you get an unduplicated audience of 32 million adults and a rating of 22.7—larger than Maude, Phyllis, or The Six Million Dollar Man. When you confine it to men 18 to 49, the rating jumps to 30.7. Which beats any regular prime-time TV series. Yet you can buy *Newsweek* at a cost per thousand for men 18–49 that's actually less than that of the average prime time show. And you can even buy the *Newsweek* plus *Time* combination at a cost per thousand that's comparable—particularly when you consider the quality of the audience. Here the picture gets still brighter. With *Newsweek* plus *Time*—or *Newsweek* plus *Sports Illustrated* or *Business Week*—you zero in on people you just can't reach that efficiently with television alone. As study after study shows, newsweekly readers are younger, better educated, more affluent. They do more. They buy more. And something else we suspect is true, they're more receptive to what a good, persuasive ad is saying. Because it's seen within the informative context of a newsweekly instead of flashing by during a break in the entertainment on TV. These days with rising costs and limited availabilities, a lot of advertisers are having some second thoughts about television. If you're among them, remember: the ratings point to the newsweeklies. For the advertiser whose budget is limited, *Newsweek* with its lower cost per thousand, is the more efficient. But consider the advantages of both. *Newsweek* plus *Time*. It's a mighty big buy.

Sound familiar? These are the same arguments that led to the destruction of so many magazines in the past. Maybe *Newsweek* feels the time is right for another battle. I think it's a mistake, because magazines and television are just too different to compare—apples and oranges, class and mass. By doing so, magazines destroy their own uniqueness, the very quality that permitted them to survive against television in the first place.

Not only did magazines survive, but new ones arrived on the scene and are prospering. If necessity is the mother of invention, television is (ironically) the unwitting father of a vital new magazine business. Television gave birth, for example, to the largest circulation magazine in America today, *TV Guide*. It's also at least partly responsible for the resurgence of the venerable old *Readers Digest*, a magazine that for years and years supported itself on circulation income alone, and accepted no advertising. Therefore, the great battle for advertising revenue against TV affected the *Digest* not at all—until one day it perceived a hole in the market where mass magazines used to be. Soon after, the *Readers Digest* opportunistically opened its pages to advertisers, and enjoyed an unexpected but welcome boom in advertising revenue.

TV also inspired a raft of other magazines that didn't compete with it for mass circulation. These are the new local magazines that deal with local issues, and that attract a concentration of more educated, sophisticated, affluent followers than TV can command. You'll find these magazines in New York, of course, but also in Atlanta, Baltimore, Boston, Charlotte, Chicago, Cincinnati, Cleveland, Dayton, Denver, Detroit, Dallas, Louisville, Los Angeles, Miami, Nashville, New Orleans, Palm Springs, Philadelphia, Phoenix, Pittsburgh, St. Louis, San Antonio, San

Diego, San Francisco, and Washington, D.C. This list doesn't even begin to consider the many smaller communities. Magazines are cropping up everywhere, from Irvine, California, to Westchester County, New York.

The magazines that died were the mass, general magazines. Those that survived and are still thriving are selective. Today magazines can compete with television on the basis of selectivity of audience and subject matter. Take the women's magazines: *Family Circle, Woman's Day, Ladies' Home Journal, McCall's, Good Housekeeping, Redbook,* and *Cosmopolitan.* And consider the men's magazines: *Playboy, Oui, Penthouse, Gallery, Esquire, True,* and *Sports Illustrated.*

That's only the beginning. There are business magazines: *Forbes, Fortune, Business Week.* There are high fashion magazines: *Vogue, Glamour, Mademoiselle, Harper's Bazaar.* Stop by any newsstand and choose from a wide selection of decorating magazines: *House Beautiful, House & Garden, Better Homes & Gardens, American Home.* Or read the news as seen by *Newsweek, Time,* or *U.S. News & World Report.* The arts, political affairs, science, literature, ecology—you name it, there's a magazine for every special interest, from *Money* (a new one) to *Popular Mechanics* (started in 1902): *Harper's, Psychology Today, New Yorker, National Geographic,* and *Scientific American.*

Magazines like these survive and coexist with television just because of their selectivity. In strict fairness, television can be selective, too. Through television, an advertiser can aim his message to the exact audience he wants by running the commercial at a certain time of day, or during a certain kind of program. Daytime TV gets a high concentration of women, for example, and sports shows draw male viewers. Every show on every network can supply a prospective advertiser with statistics that prove how many are watching and who they are by sex, age, income, geography, occupation, and much more. These numbers are compiled by an outside auditing firm known as the A. C. Nielsen Company. Shows live or die by their Nielsen ratings, because they help advertisers select only the most promising programs to wrap around their commercials.

Interestingly, a new mass general magazine is emerging, and its basic concept is not so very different from that of the defunct *Life* or *Look*. It's a picture magazine of people named, appropriately, *People*. It seems to be catching on with readers *and* advertisers. It may be the only magazine to challenge TV for the general mass audience and stay alive. Could it be that the time is ripe for a renaissance of the general mass magazine? I hope so.

Magazines are alive and well. We can all be thankful, because whenever a publication dies, the people lose another voice. And we need all the voices we can get—pro and con, consenting and dissenting. To me, the demise of a publication is like the death of a brilliant orator who presents with strength and articulation the views of his constituents. It's a loss for all people of all views when that voice is silenced.

Especially when that voice belongs to a newspaper.

Newspapers take more controversial stands on issues than magazines. They are certainly more controversial than television stations, which represent safe, neutral positions to their broad, general audience. Taking a stand, even when it creates controversy, is one of the primary roles of a newspaper. It was for newspapers' very protection that the doctrine of freedom of the press was written into our Constitution.

How did newspapers fare against TV? Although newspapers are mostly local, with self-limited relatively small circulations, they too found themselves in the path of television's momentum. Not only could "spot" TV be as local as any daily newspaper, but with all the national advertising dollars being funneled into the new medium there was less money left over for newspapers. National advertising linage began to fall off. And that put the handwriting on the wall.

National advertising is the most profitable for newspapers to carry, since it commands a higher line rate than local or retail advertising. With ad revenue down and the cost of material and labor up, newspapers found themselves in big trouble. It was survival of the fittest all over the nation. In New York, the fittest happened to be *The News, The Times,* and *The Post;* gone forever are *The Herald-Tribune, The Mirror, The World-Telegram & Sun,* and *The Journal-American.* In cities all across the country, it seemed as if more than one newspaper was a luxury. Weaker newspapers began dropping like paper airplanes. To make matters worse, local TV stations wooed and won local retail advertisers who wanted to get in on the excitement of TV.

The newspapers that survived are stronger for the experience. And so is America. The advertisers are stronger too, because strong, local papers are the primary and most essential communication link to the thinking and buying public.

JUST as magazines and newspapers changed to accommodate to television, so have advertisers' views of how to use them. Today magazines are used not only to launch entire campaigns, but very often in support of a campaign originally introduced on TV. Take, for example, the recent ad for Memorex Recording Tape, which pictures the same shattering glass demonstration used so effectively on television (see Chapter 10). You know the one: Ella Fitzgerald shatters a glass with her voice, then her recorded voice on Memorex Tape duplicates the feat. In print, the illustration shows the glass shattering twice, once during the original demonstration and once from the recorded playback. The headline asks, "Is it live, or is it Memorex?" Then the copy runs with the ball: "We proved it on our latest television commercial with Ella Fitzgerald. Whatever Ella can do, Memorex with MRX2 Oxide can do. Even shatter a glass."

To my way of thinking that's a good, intelligent use of magazine space.

Newspapers are particularly well-suited and used today as a promotional vehicle for the deliverance of a price-off store-redeemed or mail-in coupon. Look for these coupons on your newspaper's best food day, when your paper is packed with local food-chain ads, the perfect environment for shopping.

Happily for newspapers, nobody's figured out a way to deliver a coupon into a viewer's hand through a television tube.

Large budget advertisers, of course, use all media synergistically for different purposes. Michael Ephron, media director of Scali, McCabe, Sloves advertising agency, was quoted in *The New York Times Magazine* explaining his media strategy for the $10 million Volvo automobile account:

> Magazines fulfill the primary function of letting us provide someone in the market for a new car with a wealth of pertinent information. TV offers us a chance to maintain awareness of our product among the public at large, even though they're not in the market. Newspapers are an excellent retail medium—the closest one to the point of sale—we can get in dealer listings. We decided on a mix that was 50 percent TV, 35 percent magazines, and 15 percent newspapers.

In other words, television for mass. Magazines for selectivity. Newspapers for retail.

WHAT was the impact of the television revolution on the people who create advertising for all media?

Disastrous.

With the growth of television, a whole new breed of creative people emerged. They looked different. They talked differently. They dressed differently—in jeans and long hair and beads and beards; they spoke a language of their own, a cross between hip and Hollywood.

And that's where they came from, in the figurative sense. Hollywood. Eager to cash in on the new entertainment craze sweeping the world, and the advertising world in particular. This new breed thought entertainment was the objective of all advertising. The more entertaining the commercial, the better advertising it must be.

Who was to argue with them? Because they were paid incredible salaries, salaries all out of proportion to their worth, by an industry hungry for people to show how this scary new medium should be used. And the new creatives thought it beneath them to learn anything about advertising. Does one ask Lina Wertmuller to cut her teeth on trade ads, promotion pieces, brochures, packages, instructional booklets, catalogs, or point-of-purchase displays? Should a budding genius be required to finish up ads created by experienced senior people? What are you, crazy or something?

It didn't bother them that they didn't understand marketing objectives. That they couldn't write a creative strategy or reposition a product. (It takes an ad man, not a showman, to change the end benefit of a product in order to appeal to a completely new, and hopefully larger, market.) The "entertainers" looked down their creative noses at advertising people who could do all those things. They were establishment squares. Understanding the public ("those *hicks!*") was a bore, so they used themselves and their friends as representative American buyers. As a result, they turned out lousy advertising, if it was advertising at all.

It consisted of "insider" comedy, little jokes, and musical

extravaganzas that bore no more resemblance to advertising than the Grade B comedies and musicals that had nurtured them. These were dark days for advertising. For a while it looked as if the business would become an East Coast franchise of West Coast TV and movie studios. The crowning absurdity was the introduction of those obscene Academy Award-type orgies to the advertising industry. Hollywood reigned supreme.

But not forever. It took a good ten years, but gradually, professional advertising people, having solved the "mysteries" of television, wrested the business back again. And it happened not a moment too soon. There are still some show biz personalities around, but for the most part, the smarter ones who took the time to learn something along the way have prevailed. The "entertainers" are gone. The awards shows remain as their legacy, but fortunately there are fewer of those left, too.

Television dealt a heavy blow to magazines and newspapers by depriving them of large numbers of readers and huge amounts of advertising income. Some were destroyed altogether. Those that survived did so only by making adjustments and learning to live with television. Advertising, too, had to adjust to the new medium and learn to use it best. The learning period was long and painful, but the message is now clear: the medium is *not* the message.

Television not only came close to destroying magazines and newspapers, it damn near killed advertising as well!

To me, print is the purest form of advertising. It pits the creative mind one-on-one against a blank sheet of paper. With no outside influences. No tricks. No gimmicks. No hiding behind actors or music or jokes or props. When it comes to print, it's just you, that blank sheet of paper—and the moment of truth for the creative person.

Those who can meet the challenge of print are the truly gifted. Those who can't, no matter how creative they look or dress or talk, are not—and never will be—ad people. Why? Because print is the one medium (including newspapers, magazines, outdoor, even matchbooks) that separates the Simplifiers from the Complicators.

Print is the mother medium. The basic medium. So basic that it can even be used as a guide to creating better television commercials.

Turn the page and find out how.

9
How to Create Better TV Commercials

BELIEVE IT OR NOT, IT'S REALLY A LOT EASIER TO CREATE A good television commercial, than it is to create a good print ad. TV is an easy medium for a creative man. For one thing, he's got an expanse of time that he can count on—anywhere from 10 to 60 seconds. For another, he's got motion to work with, and nothing commands more attention. And he's got sound, everything from a single voice to the London Philharmonic. He's got professional actors. Producers. Directors. Editors. If he can't communicate an idea with all that going for him, well, maybe he doesn't really have an idea at all.

A print ad, on the other hand, requires real discipline because it has none of that magic going for it. No time sequence. No motion. No voice, music, or effects. All you've got is a piece of paper and some printing ink. And from that, you've got to create something that will attract someone's attention, entice him to read your words (an act requiring effort, unlike the passive business of watching and listening), communicate the selling idea, and then convince him to try the product.

That's tough. Much tougher than creating a TV commercial.

That's why I tend to judge the conceptual thinking ability of the writers and art directors I've interviewed, beginners and old pros alike, by their print ads. I'm convinced that anybody who can create good print ads can create good TV advertising, even if he's never done it before. Conversely, it doesn't always follow that someone with a proven track record in TV advertising can create good print; it's been my experience that those with a background of heavy TV lack the sharp, disciplined thinking of writers who started out by writing print ad after print ad after print ad, first trade and then consumer. The same is true of art directors.

You don't believe me? Let me describe the kind of person who comes looking for a job with a portfolio full of film and a few, grudging print ads. His thinking is fuzzy. He can't isolate a single salient point—or make one quickly. He thinks in terms of scenarios instead of sentences that have beginnings, middles, and ends. He makes vast plans for lighting, casting, camera angles, ECU's (that's Extreme Close-Up in TV jargon, part of a huge lexicon of initials meant to intimidate the poor average ad person, and a language I've never bothered to learn) and a whole panoply of other techniques long before he ever has a real idea. Give him a print ad to do and he's lost. Utterly lost. I feel like Simon Legree even asking a guy like this to describe in a single, succinct sentence the basic selling idea behind a commercial he's worked on. Precision isn't his bag.

He's in show biz.

Now picture the guy who comes to me with a satchel full of great print ads and no TV. It usually turns out that once he starts working in TV, he finds it so much easier than what he's been doing that he creates the best TV commercials in the place. They'll be crisper, cleaner, fresher, simpler, and more convincing than those being turned out by the so-called TV pros. He may not be familiar with the techniques or the nomenclature, but he knows how to think and how to communicate the results of his thinking quickly and clearly. It's easy to teach a new technique to someone who thinks. What's hard is trying to teach a master of technique a new way to think.

Right at this point I'd like to defend myself against all the TV specialists who are crying "foul" because I seem to be boosting print at the expense of their beloved medium. Not true. I no more believe in the intrinsic fuzziness of all TV creative thinking than I believe that all print people are necessarily masters of decisiveness. A smart person is a smart person in any situation. Just as a good ad man is a good ad man in any medium. He'll create good advertising in print, TV, radio, outdoor, direct mail, skywriting, matchbooks—you name it, if he's smart, he'll do it well. What concerns me here is the dangerous likelihood that we will get more medium than message from creative people who have concentrated on TV to the exclusion of every other medium. Too many of our creative people are more in love with TV technique than advertising, and as a result too much of today's TV advertising is entertaining, witty, funny—and pointless.

What is it about the magical medium that calls forth the C. B. DeMille in us, anyway? I'm not just talking about TV ad people whose hearts are really in show business. I've watched good print creative people whom I've seen think simply and clearly under normal circumstances metamorphose into temperamental, paranoid, raving maniacs on a TV set. Gone are the quiet, decisive habits of mind that made them good ad people in the first place. Quite simply, they've been seduced by the new-found wonders of TV technique, by the intensity a big-budget project demands, by the glamour of make-up men scurrying around a celebrity. Hoards of other professionals watching them as they create. Grips and gaffers, electricians and carpenters, cameramen and sound technicians ready to spring into action at their every word. The immediacy of enforced teamwork, so different from the lonely evenings spent perspiring over a manual typewriter or set of multicolored magic markers to produce a great print ad. In a way, the pinwheel eyes and megalomania on the set are all very understandable, but it's the commercial result that suffers. And that's dangerous.

So I've spent some years working out a modest proposal for saving our good and righteous ad people from the forbidden lures of Madame TV. I can't guarantee success for it 100 percent of the time, but it works for me and a lot of other people who now use it to turn out some outstanding TV work. I hope it turns out to be a trend that spreads.

If Marshall McLuhan is right in believing that intelligence begins with the ability to condense, then intelligent advertising should begin with the ability to condense a complicated sales message down to its basic form: a headline and a picture. The further away we get from these two elements, the poorer our communication becomes. So, far from being ends in themselves, TV techniques should operate only to make the headline and picture more interesting, more exciting, and more convincing as clearly, quickly, and simply as possible.

With that in mind, I ask you to consider my plan: Every creative team, before starting a TV campaign or commercial, should first rough out a print ad communicating the same message to be communicated in the TV commercial. Needless to say, the team should execute this print ad, consisting of headline, rough visual, and copy points, just for themselves. No one else should see it. To be on the safe side, they should also consider several approaches before deciding on the best way to go. In the end, it's not only conceivable but entirely probable that they'll spend more time on the ad than on the actual television storyboard, because the storyboard will come easily after this basic conceptual groundwork has been laid.

If nothing else, this technique is bound to sharpen creative thinking by forcing a team to determine, first, the single most important point to be made, and, second, how best to make it.

As for the rest, it's easy. The print ad should be used as a blueprint for the TV storyboard and the final execution. All along the way, the storyboard should be judged against this ad to see that the idea hasn't been lost, obscured, or slowed down in translation from print to TV. And it would be a good idea if, in the final production of the commercial, the print ad were prominently displayed so that every time a production technique begins to crush the basic idea, it can be stopped then and there.

As a guide for the final editing, nothing could beat the print ad. It should also be compared to the finished commercial, just to see how closely the techniques of one medium has approximated the other.

The print ad, you might say, is ideally suited to serve as the conscience of our industry. If we paid more attention to our consciences, as theologians and thinkers have advised for solid centuries, we would see better and more effective TV commercials in the future.

I can guarantee it.

10

The Demo–
TV's Ultimate Weapon

TELEVISION WAS MADE FOR DEMONSTRATIONS.

And that's very fortunate, because nothing achieves believability like a good, simple, relevant demonstration. Why? Because a mere claim of product performance or superiority told in words and pictures, no matter how earthshaking in concept or perfectly realized in execution, is just one more claim among thousands competing for the consumers' credence. As such, a claim will be accepted or rejected by the viewer almost at whim, and most whims are inclined to be negative.

A good solid demo, on the other hand, is proof positive of the claim made. It lifts that claim out of the controversial world of opinion and positions it firmly within the realm of absolute fact.

Of course, there are demonstrations and demonstrations, and the use of this technique is not an automatic guarantee of believability. Some recent demos I've seen, for example, have demonstrated an irrelevant or inconsequential feature. No one will care (or buy) unless the feature demonstrated offers a substantial advantage. Other demos simply do not prove their sales point convincingly, and some get so complicated that they lose their believability.

I insist upon seven basic ingredients for making good, convincing demonstrations:

1. *Make it interesting, exciting, suspenseful or dramatic.* I'm talking about execution here, and everything I said about execution in Chapter 3 still goes. Execution is the soul mate of your concept. It's what keeps your audience in their seats when their favorite show breaks for a commercial. It's the setting that displays your jewel of an idea to perfection, so prepare it with care.

I point again to the classic Sears power mower commercial that combined a simple, believable demonstration with an element of uncontrived suspense to make a near-flawless sales point with maximum impact. A live commercial, you'll recall, it demonstrated the easy starting capability of the Sears mower as the mower started up almost every time the test was run. A tally of successes and failures was kept throughout the campaign right on screen, and if the score was less than perfect, it was close enough and honest enough to be convincing.

But nothing could top that split-second of suspense falling between the activation of the starter and the answering roar of the motor. Would it make it? Would the mower prove itself on live television, where precious little can be faked, or would it flop, die, and see its failure recorded in big, black letters on the public tally?

Now that's exciting—a critical feature of the product demonstrated on live TV in a manner guaranteed to stop a viewer in his tracks when he's on the way to the refrigerator.

2. *Make sure it's relevant to the point you want to make.* To do this, you've got to think *hard* about what you're trying to say, then make your demo accomplish exactly that. No frills. No show biz. No laughs. Just a single-minded sprint for the finish.

Consider Fruit of the Loom pantyhose. The Unique Advantage they tried to advertise when they first hit the market was sheerness. So they created a commercial that featured a pretty girl talking about her pantyhose, its strength, and particularly its sheerness. An ordinary commercial, up to that point. Suddenly, her pitch completed, the girl walks toward the camera, removes a pair of pantyhose from the lens, and reveals to us that the entire commercial had been shot through it. Yet the quality of the picture was no sharper or clearer after the pantyhose had been removed.

Now that's a great demonstration of the very point they wanted to make—sheerness—and one that never strayed from the central point of the commercial.

Another was the IBM Correcting Selectric typewriter spot that accomplished, almost without audio, everything that a great demonstration should. As for suiting the demo to the main point, this one gets an A plus, because the entire message of the commercial is typed by the product.

It begins by typing WATCH CAREFULOY. The typewriter then goes back to correct the spelling error, changing the "O" to an "L" automatically with no erasure. The rest of the commercial's message is then typed with one more spelling error along the way, which is promptly corrected by the automatic typewriter.

Have you ever seen a more believable demonstration of a product's Unique Advantage? Or one in which the feature sells itself? A relevant demonstration eliminates the need for much explanation, and self-explanatory commercials *sell*.

3. *Prove your point conclusively.* Some people, when telling an anecdote to illustrate an important point, drop the ball on the two-yard line by failing to make the moral of the story sufficiently clear. To them, and to everyone who has ever labored over the creation of a demo, I offer the following object lesson in proving a point:

Two short pieces of board are glued together right before our eyes with Elmer's, then put in place at a pool for use as a diving board. Then, in a demonstration that had me cringing in my seat almost afraid to look, a diver jumps up and down on this glued board to show how firmly the pieces adhere. The commercial ends with a great line that points out that Elmer's is stronger glue than you'll ever need for most household jobs.

And how about this recent commercial for Master Lock? A marksman using a high-powered rifle fires at a Master Lock. Bull's-eye! Slow-motion photography dramatizes the tremendous damage done to the lock at the instant of impact. Yet the lock will not open even when forced.

Conclusive? Absolutely. To the point? Utterly. Proof? Positive.

4. *Keep the staging uncontrived.* This is a toughie. Because the temptation is to think that the bigger and more elaborate the demonstration is, the more resounding the proof.

Not so.

Take a look at this lovely bit of simplicity sponsored by J. C. Penney's Flexxtra pantyhose. A model crams both her legs into one leg of Flexxtra pantyhose, and it stretches to accommodate them. Then she removes one leg and the pantyhose snaps back and snugly embraces the remaining leg. A superb demonstration that proves how elastic and impervious to sags and bags Flexxtras are.

More important than this, though, is the fact that all it

required to stage this extremely effective demonstration was a pair of legs and a single pantyhose garment.

Think about *that*.

5. *Be sure it's simple to follow and understand.* Even if the concept is more complicated than you would like, you'd be surprised at how simply it can be demonstrated. Like this one: The drawing of an eye appears on screen and becomes filled with all the air pollutants that irritate it during the course of a day—smoke, smut, pollen, et cetera. Then Murine is dropped into the eye. At once, the pollutants are washed away and are replaced with a fresh, clean daisy.

There's an awful lot going on in this commercial, to be sure, but the procession of ideas is orderly and easy to follow. It doesn't take an Einstein to grasp the simple, solid point it makes ("Murine gets the red out"), and no one is going to die of boredom in the process, either.

In all, it illustrates how a demonstration must flow—and not stumble—if it is to be believed.

6. *Make it preemptive.* By this I simply mean that a demonstration, if it is to be any good at all, must be so memorable, and so closely identified with your product, that no one would *dare* use it after you've done it.

Not a soul would advertise "squeezability" in connection with a bathroom tissue after the Mr. Whipple Charmin series, for example, nor is another paper towel going to get away with a crumpled towel-in-glass absorbancy demonstration as performed by Nancy Walker for Bounty.

Demonstrations become preemptive if they've been fashioned with enough originality. Certainly Wesson oil has the idea of frying a crustless loaf of bread all sewn up; yet this demonstration grew out of a simple desire to show that the product won't make fried foods soggy inside, a point every oil manufacturer is anxious to make. The commercial shows a loaf of white bread being fried in Wesson. It gets golden well-done on the outside, but a knife cuts into the bread to reveal that the inside is still soft and fluffy.

The same goes for Heinz ketchup. Nobody but *nobody* is going to promote "slowness" as a virtue of ketchup after Heinz has used it in demonstration after demonstration to illustrate the richness and thickness of their product.

7. *A demonstration must be believable beyond the shadow of a doubt.* And that means you've got to see the point proved before your very eyes, and have absolute faith in the method of proof.

Let me give you an example. Some years back Du Pont did a commercial that I never forgot. For total believability, this one got me hook, line, and sinker. The product was the FE 1301 Fire Extinguisher Vapor, and they demonstrated it by placing an announcer in a chair located in the middle of a huge studio. Ostensibly his job is to deliver the message about this new fire extinguishing vapor developed for installation in plants and factories, but suddenly a highly combustible liquid (presumably gasoline) is poured in a circle around his chair and ignited. Immediately it bursts into a roaring ring of fire that hungrily licks at the area between itself and the announcer's chair. When a whoosh of the Du Pont vapor is released, the menacing fire is snuffed out.

Our cool announcer then informs us that not only does the vapor "Stop fire dead in its tracks, but it can't get going again." To demonstrate, he tries unsuccessfully to light a match, all the while assuring us that there's enough air for him to breathe and escape, but not enough to allow the fire to start again. One match fails. The second fails. The third sputters but fails. A few are lit at once, but fail. Who could ever forget or doubt the claims made for the Du Pont FE 1301 vapor after witnessing this demonstration? And what could be more convincing in a demo than a man who risks his life on the results? That has to be the ultimate demonstration.

And the ultimate in believability, too.

Maybe I'm naive, but I don't see how they could have faked this demonstration. Nor can I figure out how the Memorex people did another memorable demo except by total honesty. In that one, an operatic tenor shatters a glass by hitting a high note while his voice is recorded on a Memorex cassette. When the tape is played back, a second glass is shattered by the recording, proving that Memorex records and plays back original sounds with magnificent fidelity.

You can't beat that for believability. And if you think I told it before, you're right. Memorex told the same story in print using Ella Fitzgerald. (They also used her on TV.)

COMMERCIALS like these are good for our consciences. To the escapades of all those Hollywood hotshots, they say, "Hey! Stop the nonsense! *This* is what advertising's all about!" There is damned little showmanship involved in any of these commercials. No casts of thousands. No tricky camera angles, special effects, jingles, dancing girls. There is not one thickening plot. No saccharine "slice of life" situation comedies. Not even a single funny line. Just good show-and-tell demonstration.

Yet I found them more engrossing, more interesting, and more suspenseful than any of the engineered hilarity that passes for advertising on television today.

Long live the demo. Long live effective, believable advertising.

11

Comparison, Fear, Naming Names, and Simulation

IF THERE WERE AN EASIER ROAD TO BELIEVABILITY THAN the standard show-and-tell commercial you can bet I'd take it.

In fact, I'd even be willing to stand up before the nation on TV and tell everyone just how wonderful my clients' products are. (At least one agency president has already done that.) One look at my winsome smile and sincere, catch-in-the-throat delivery and you'd trip over your own feet getting out the door to buy the product, right?

Wrong. And that's why commercials are so hard to write. It's not enough that they be sincere, they have to make you *believe*—somehow, anyhow, or they're no good at all.

So how does a commercial achieve believability when the audience and the teller of the story are divided by thousands of miles, millions of dollars worth of technical equipment, and scores of executives and creative people who have re-shaped, refined, edited, and re-edited the message every inch along the way?

It's easy. You simply pick the technique that will do the

most convincing job for your product, letting it display the product to full advantage, like a picture frame. There are so many techniques to choose from that I can't really list them all here. But I've done the next best thing by narrowing the possibilities down to four that are tried and true routes to believability. And to reenforce my point, I won't just *tell* you how well they work. I'll *show* you how they've lent credence to commercials you've watched on your own living room set.

1. *Comparison commercials:* Right in the middle of Marcus Welby, with the diagnosis of a lingering, tropical disease tantalizingly near, your screen becomes dark, then lightens into a shot of two neighbors carrying their garbage out to the curb for collection. It's early morning and both men are dressed in business suits for the office. One of them, though, is struggling with a big, heavy, dirty old garbage can that overflows with refuse. The other is nonchalantly holding a clean, compact bag in one hand. The announcer explains that both the compact bag and the full garbage pail contain one week's accumulation of garbage.

Obviously one of those guys has it pretty easy, and it doesn't take a wizard to figure out what part the Sears Kenmore compactor played. I think this is a sensational commercial that builds believability for its product by dramatizing the end result of using the product and comparing it to the end result of not using it, or of using another product. It's true that the commercial fails to sell the "unique features" of the Sears Kenmore compactor in a competitive manner; instead it seems to be selling the entire category of compactors. Sears no doubt feels the consumer compactor is so virgin a category that any advertising will help it, and that the Sears product will gain a major share of that business. I don't know that for sure, but it seems a pretty good guess.

I *do* know, however, that this commercial gets an A plus for believability because it contrasts what the product can do with a less attractive alternative. The resulting conclusion is total believability. And that is advertising—real advertising.

Let's look at another example of the same technique: the old Shell gas Platformate tests. Remember those? Essentially, they demonstrated the superior mileage performance of cars running on Shell with Platformate, a compelling, believable, hard-selling concept. The best of the lot followed two cars circling the island of Manhattan. All the circumstances are identical except the brand of gasoline. One doesn't make it all the way around, but the other makes it clear to the Staten Island Ferry—because it runs on Shell containing Platformate. To me, by the way, this simple "A is better than B" demonstration is all the more believable because it takes place in an everyday driving situation I can identify with instead of some salt flat where exotic racing cars are tested.

Comparison lends itself nicely to the advertising of packaged goods, too. Consider the Light Powder Arrid deodorant commercial of some years ago that opened with a voice-over announcing: "I'm going to try something nutty" (an apologetic line the commercial could have done without). A man sprays ordinary deodorant on one arm, puts a cotton ball on it, then turns his arm over so the cotton is dangling from his arm. "Aaaahhhhh," muses the announcer gratuitously, "It's sticky."

Now he tries the same thing on his other arm, using Light Powder Arrid for the spraying. Of course the cotton ball falls off because (as the announcer carefully explains) light powder isn't sticky.

In spite of a few sticky lines, the commercial makes an excellent point: nonsticky Arrid powder won't cause your clothes to stick to you. You've seen it with your own eyes and judged between the two with your own brain. Now do you believe in Arrid?

You bet.

Just for good measure, take another look at what the comparison technique can do for an inexpensive, frequently purchased and highly competitive product like potato chips. Two plain brown paper bags appear before the camera, one filled with ordinary potato chips and the other with Chipos brand. They are allowed to sit for a couple of hours until it becomes obvious that the bag containing regular chips is spotting badly with grease stains. The Chipos bag, on the other hand, is almost as clean as it was when it was placed there. Now do you believe Chipos when they say their potato chips are almost grease free? And which chip would you rather put in your mouth? This is a simple, effective commercial that puts the evidence before your eyes and invites you to compare. People believe in comparisons, and when they believe, they buy.

2. *Fear in commercials:* A garage mechanic speaks to us as he replaces a car's engine. He says it cost about $400 to do the job. Then he holds up a Fram oil filter and says it costs $4. If the car's owner had changed the oil filter often enough, he wouldn't need a new engine now. "The choice is yours," shrugs the mechanic, with chilling insouciance. "Pay me now or pay me later."

I find this commercial to be devastatingly believable. I'm afraid *not* to believe it, or to tempt fate by neglecting my oil filter until a new engine is needed. Like the Sears compactor commercial, this campaign is selling generically instead of specifically (a practice I usually oppose), but a look at the statistics would show that Fram is a major factor in replacement oil filters in those areas where the commercial was run, making generic sell good strategy.

With skillfully pointed commercials like this one, they could scarcely miss.

Fear sells softer goods than oil filters, too. Take the terrific American Express commercials that demonstrated all the ways in which you can be relieved of your money. One showed a lecture and demonstration in a school for pickpockets. It was hairy to overhear someone making plans to rob me. In another commercial, I learned how a sexy woman in a bikini is used as a decoy on a beach while her companion lifts wallets from an appreciative audience of oglers. It's scary. It's also believable and promotes belief in the necessity of the product.

"*Don't* believe," these commercials seem to be saying, "and see what happens."

I'd rather believe.

3. *Naming names:* I'm in favor of telling the world that your product is superior to your competitor's if that superiority can be proved. So it's only a step from that premise to naming your competitor and showing his product losing out to yours. Now *that's* believability!

We're watching a procession of foreign cars wind up a narrow mountain road in single file. The Capri starts from way back in the pack and then pulls out of the lane to pass car after car, sounding its little toylike horn in double beeps each time it passes a competitor. Finally it moves into second spot behind a Volkswagen. All the while, the announcer has been naming the cars the Capri has passed—Jaguar, Mercedes-Benz, Rolls-Royce, Volvo, et cetera—and concludes that in two years, Capri has passed every European import in sales except one. (He also touches upon Capri's most attractive features, like radial tires and rack-and-pinion steering, while he's at it.) The commercial ends with the Capri beeping its horn impatiently at the VW.

What makes this a great, totally believable commercial? The fact that people believe commercials that mention competitors' names, that's what. They assume (and not without justification) that what gets said about the competitor's product must be true or it wouldn't be aired on TV. What's more, they know you'd be sued for your last nickel by your competitor if you bent the truth by so much as a hair.

A commercial that names names achieves a level of believability that the one making unilateral claims for its product can't reach. A noncompetitive commercial is always subject to a great deal of skepticism. A competitive commercial, on the other hand, is rarely questioned when presented in an honest, factual way.

Is there anyone who would doubt the claim that Capri is the second largest-selling European car sold in America after seeing this commercial?

I doubt it.

Another example of how well competitive advertising sells is the Marcal Sofpac toilet tissue ad of a few seasons back. It opened with a shot of an optometrist's eye chart. The camera eye then looked at the chart through a sheet of Charmin toilet tissue (yes, it was identified by name), but the eye chart was still perfectly visible through it. When a sheet of Marcal was placed in front of the camera lens instead, the chart couldn't be read at all.

The announcer explained that we couldn't see through Marcal because it's doubled. He concluded by pointing out the obvious: "If you can see through your tissue, maybe you should switch to one you can't see through." Even though this commercial made the same mistake of selling 2-ply toilet tissue generically instead of telling us why Marcal is the *one* 2-ply toilet tissue to buy, it sure made a valid point against Charmin, the market leader. Once you've seen this commercial, you really believe that Marcal has it all over Charmin. And you don't have to squeeze it to believe it.

4. *Simulation:* If I told you that a certain exercise salon in town could whittle you down to an attractive size, would you believe me? You might, but you'd believe me much faster if I illustrated that statement with a convincing visual.

Nu-Dimension Figure Salons did just that. For total believability, nothing could be better than watching a fat woman (through a series of time sequences called match dissolves) shed inches and trim down to a slim, trim shape right before your eyes. A before-and-after sequence would be great too. But unhappily both these techniques are next to impossible to get on the air because of federal code restrictions.

So Nu-Dimension did the next best thing: it simulated its story. The commercial began with a paper doll that simulates a woman. At first the paper doll is a big, hefty-looking one, but it's slowly trimmed down with a pair of scissors to a very sexy silhouette. The point, of course, is that this figure salon will cut you down to size. And while the simulation doesn't approach the believability level of using a live woman, it sure does make the point simply and unmistakably.

Sometimes simulation can make a point that a film sequence can't. For instance, a Bumble Bee salmon commercial of some years ago opened with a shot of a salmon leaping out of the water and hurling itself upstream. Only it wasn't really a live fish. It was a can. A can of Bumble Bee salmon. For 60 seconds the can sliced through currents, fought against rapids, leaped over waterfalls and, finally, swam into a net and got yanked from the deep. Behind all this simulation is a sound concept: inside every Bumble Bee salmon can is a very, very, fresh fish indeed. I might not believe that when a spokesman tells me so, but watching the can flash through the water helps.

Pittsburgh Latex house paint did something similar when they used simulation to prove a point that might have been botched horribly by a real film sequence. To illustrate the fact that houses must be able to breathe freely and easily through the paint applied to them, Pittsburgh simulated a breathing house by distorting the video to represent inhaling and exhaling in synchronization with the sounds of heavy, labored breathing. It certainly was unique, and it illustrated the concept as no other technique could have. When it was over, I really believed that Pittsburgh paint wouldn't smother my house. Maybe that fact will occur to me next time I go to buy paint.

THAT'S really what it's all about, you know, getting those prospects to believe you enough to try the product. Because we're not in the believability business to tell consumers what good guys we are. That's public relations, not advertising. We just want to make a credible point that will stick in the prospect's mind at the checkout counter. No matter what he remembers about your commercial—whether it's a breathing house, a cotton ball adhering to a sticky arm, a timeless copy slogan or a back-to-back comparison of products—first, last, and always he must believe your message. Comparison, fear, naming names, and simulation are all persuasive techniques that lead to believability.

12
How <u>Not</u> to Use a Testimonial

I DON'T KNOW ABOUT YOU, BUT IT TAKES A BIT MORE THAN some famous star's say-so to convince me of a product's intrinsic merit. I'm not as easily impressed as I once was, and the days when I might have rented Don Rickles' favorite cars just for the hell of it are as remote as the stories in a yellowing issue of *Photoplay*. These days, I demand a good solid switching idea before I'll try *anything*, even from a spokesperson whose face is as familiar to me as that of an old and trusted friend.

After all, I expect more of my friends than charisma. I expect the honest truth.

That's why I tend to devote something less than full, rapt attention to commercials using famous people as crutches. Like the recent spot that teamed the Wizard of Avis with actor Jack Palance, for example. Palance starts off all right, outlining some of the problems that the Wizard of Avis can solve for car renters, but then the camera swings from him to a pretty, smiling Avis girl who rhapsodizes over the Avis system of computerized reservations. Except for those brief, introductory remarks, Jack Palance is neither seen nor heard from again.

What a waste! This is simply no way to use a celebrity! When professional announcers can be had for the asking, why push a famous actor into the role? Not only did Palance fail to add anything to the commercial, he actually detracted from it to the extent that I spent most of the Avis girl's time on camera busily trying to figure out what important mission Palance was supposed to have accomplished. So don't ask me anything about the Avis system of computerized reservations; like so many who saw the commercial, I was too busy puzzling over the spokesman to catch any of the critical sales points.

None of this is meant to be critical of Mr. Palance, by the way. It's not his fault that he wasn't used correctly. But someone failed to make him a functional part of the commercial, and as a result, he stuck out like a sore thumb. And a very expensive one.

If I may invoke Seiden's Law again for a moment, I'd like to do some rapid finger-counting to pinpoint what this commercial *cost* in relation to what it *yields*. I don't have any idea of Jack Palance's fee for this commercial, but I happen to know that stars of top magnitude have lately been commanding a million dollars for their commercial appearances. I'm not saying Jack Palance got a million, but whatever he got, it was more than the part they gave him to do was worth.

The commercial was totally unbelievable. How could it have been believable when Mr. Palance's part in it was part of the unbelievability?

To have any value at all, a spokesperson must be believable or at least uniquely suited to a particular situation, product, or strategy. David Janssen is a big flop as an Excedrin spokesman, in my opinion, because we have no reason for believing in him as a medical expert. (Do you think he might have been hired as spokesman because he played the part of an ex-doctor in "The Fugitive" all those years ago? I can't for the life of me think of any other reason.) Jack Benny, on the other hand, was a particularly fine spokesman for any kind of economy-oriented product or service because of his comic personna as a miser. Dina Merrill would be a fine spokeswoman for a luxury product, Jack Klugman or Phyllis Diller for anything that promises to make your life a little more orderly, Tony Randall would be excellent for a grooming product, Raquel Welch for cosmetics, and so on down the line. But Jack Palance is neither believable nor appropriate for Avis unless the commercial makes a connection between the actor and the service. And it doesn't.

All of which leads me to believe that there are a few simple rules that advertisers *must* observe when using spokespeople for commercial testimonials, lest the commercial and the product suffer a loss of credibility.

First, advertisers must realize that an endorsement is only as good as the believability of the endorser.

Second, the endorser must be appropriate to the product endorsed.

Third, the endorser should never be allowed to overpower the endorsement.

Finally, there's one even more vital question: Is the personality really needed at all? Will he add credibility to the commercial? Does the commercial work just as well, or maybe better, without the personality? Such a celebrity can make a good commercial great, but he or she can never make a bad commercial good—just more expensive. This is why, sometimes, it's infinitely preferable to skip the famous-name celebrity altogether and turn the testimonial over to another kind of spokesperson . . . the unknown (but knowing) expert.

Why? Because the point of all this testifying is to make the audience *believe* in something. If you, the advertiser, use a celebrity spokesperson from the unbelievable, unreal, make-believe world of show business, you risk having your audience pooh-pooh your commercial on the grounds that your show biz celebrity is just mouthing another part written for him or her. Testimonials, remember, are only believable to the extent of the specific expertise of the people who deliver them, so movie stars (unless they are attesting to some matter about which they are acknowledged experts) are usually less credible than non-celebrity experts.

This is what I mean: In a recent Chevron commercial, an automotive specialist is asked to break down an engine and guess how many miles it has gone. In the process of dismantling and studying it piece by piece, he comments on what he finds in the manner of a pathologist performing an autopsy for medical students. He observes that very little dirt has been deposited in the vital parts and, after the dissection, he estimates that the engine had traveled between 10,000 and 20,000 miles. When the specialist is told that the engine had in fact traveled 62,000 miles—fueled all the way by Chevron—he's amazed that the gasoline kept the engine so clean.

This is a great commercial because it's completely believable. The automotive expert is authentic, obviously not an actor and obviously not acting. As a result, the commercial is low key, real, and more believable than all of those Broadway musical comedies starring singing and dancing pistons, musical carburetors, and the obnoxious Mr. Dirt who fails to convince me of the very same point. With one simple (and, I daresay, inexpensive) commercial, Chevron makes its point a lot more convincingly than all the Mobil Mr. Dirt spectaculars combined.

That's what the expert testimonial is all about: believability.

Let's take another example, an RCA-TV commercial in which chief engineers of TV stations around the country are identified by name and title. As we are introduced to each, he makes a statement about TV color reception from his professional point of view. One, for instance, says that RCA delivers color comparable to that of professional monitors. Another talks about critical color tests and the conditions under which blues and reds stay true in shifting lights. Still another expert talks about reliability and color fidelity. Summing up their remarks, the announcer states that these experts *know* what color looks like. That's why they all have RCA sets at home. It reproduces the color with great fidelity and few problems. The commercial ends with the theme line stretched across the screen: "More than twice as many TV chief engineers own RCA as any other color TV." It's not a great commercial. But it's a good, solid, honest and believable one that's bound to have a tremendous impact upon anyone in the market for a new color TV set. How can they ignore all those experts? They're just too believable to be disregarded.

Can an "expert" testimonial ever make use of humor? Sure—as long as the humor doesn't detract from the sales message. Remember the Progresso spaghetti sauce commercial that sought to establish Progresso as an authentically Italian sauce? So who is more qualified to testify as an expert than a real Italian mama? This commercial showed us a series of three honest-to-goodness Italian homemakers from

Brooklyn, photographed in their own kitchens and dining rooms, each of whom urged a steaming platter of spaghetti upon us with great determination, large smiles, and wheedling cries of "Mangia!" meaning "Eat!" The voice-over says that for years Italian mothers have been serving Progresso. Now it's time for everyone to try it: "Mangia Goldberg, O'Brien, Mangia Lopez, Armstrong."

This is an awfully good commercial, combining warmth with humor properly used. But most of all, it establishes Progresso's authenticity beyond a doubt, just as an expert testimonial should. (Who should know more about authentic Italian spaghetti sauce than authentic Italian mothers?) All hail to the power of believability!

Is this to say that big-name celebrities should never be used as spokespeople if anonymous "experts" can be found? Of course not! Especially if an advertiser can find himself a celeb who can deliver a pitch with the power and panache of a David Niven or Joan Crawford for Pan American. Now *there* were a couple of testimonials!

Mind you, I first saw these commercials on a day when I was exposed to some of the then-current most nauseating, most depressing crop of commercials I had ever seen in any one Sunday of TV viewing in my life, a fact which made Joan Crawford's low-key stand-up testimonial for Pan Am all the more refreshing. Later in the same day, I was equally impressed by David Niven's male counterpart to that commercial. In a word, these two were everything a commercial testimonial should be. Simple. Sincere. Believable. Straight from the hip and right out of the "Pure and Simple" school.

What made these commercials particularly impressive was the fact that, in the face of the extravagant, no expenses spared, productions its competitors were offering, Pan Am chose to film powerful, simple, gutsy testimonials at all.

American Airlines was featuring a devastating bikini-clad woman emerging from the surf to the "Good Life," National Airlines was selling its fly-me girls, Eastern was pursuing the idea (expertly) of husbands and wives getting away together into the sun, while TWA was selling its better meals and luggage convenience under the general heading of "TWA is what travel should be." Additionally, the foreign airlines were giving Pan Am a run for its money, notably with Robert Morley's charming testimonial for BOAC. That's the kind of competition Pan Am had to reckon with. And still, Pan American chose to gamble with a couple of commercials that tell us people are afraid to fly and that point out good food and good service are secondary and expected from a major airline. What people want, the campaign concludes, is safety and experience. It's a risky strategy. But in the capable hands of its spokespeople, Pan Am's gamble paid off.

Joan Crawford simply tells us that she flies much too much to be influenced by an airline's fancy meals and plush interiors. What's more, their prices are all the same. So when she has to fly, she generally tries to fly Pan Am, the world's most experienced airline, because she's really not too crazy about flying.

And David Niven? He says he flies thousands of miles a year and he doesn't choose an airline because of cuisine or decor. "That's nonsense," he says, "and the fares are all the same anyway." So, when he has a choice, he flies the world's most experienced airline, because when it comes to flying, "that suave, sophisticated *bon vivant* David Niven is the world's most experienced . . . chicken." How's that for basic honesty and sincerity?

These commercials do exactly what a celebrity spokesperson testimonial should do: they make us believe what the spokespeople say is true. Why? Because both of these commercials are disarmingly honest and simple. Both personalities claim they fly a lot (easy enough to believe), and that they have a basic fear of flying—also easy to believe, since most people do, even seasoned travelers. So when they recommend Pan Am's expertise to us, we're predisposed to believe them. Delivered simply, against "at home" backgrounds, these commercials contain nothing that interferes with the basic sales pitch. As a result, both commercials are wholly believable. And that's the name of the game.

IN THE final analysis, a commercial is a selling vehicle that must be able to stand on its own feet, without a spokesman, before I would consider using a spokesman at all. A famous (or non-famous) spokesman cannot be the entire creative strategy, but should merely add excitement, memorability, and believability to an already sound package of sales points. A spokesman is an executional technique, not a concept. Used properly, he or she can tip the scales in favor of believability every time.

Take it from the world's most experienced Doubting Thomas.

13

How Not to Talk to a Woman

GIVEN THE MOMENTUM THE WOMEN'S RIGHTS MOVEMENT has been gathering over the past few years, it would sure be easy to open this subject with a weighty analysis of what's wrong with female-oriented advertising today. Instead, let me refer you to a Noxzema commercial of recent vintage which seems to me to be the distillation of how not to sell a woman.

The commercial pictures a beautiful girl bending over her sink. The off-screen voice asks what she's doing.

"Washing my face," she replies.

"With soap?" inquires Mr. Voice.

The girl looks up at the question in surprise. "At my age?" she asks. Surprise gives way to emphasis: "I use Noxzema."

At this point, her boyfriend enters the picture to deliver the clincher:

"So," he muses, "that's how you stay so young looking!"

I didn't know whether to laugh or cry. For one mad moment, I actually toyed with the idea that it was a big put-on concocted by the Noxzema people as a gleeful bit of self-satire.

It wasn't. They were dead serious.

Here is this beautiful young thing, who looks all of 18 and certainly no older than 25, supposedly concerned about her aging skin and revealing her secret for staying so "young looking." I know her real secret, of course: she was born in the mid-1950s.

Can you imagine how this commercial must make women viewers in their thirties, forties, and fifties feel? How they must writhe to hear from this little woman-child's own baby lips her worry about her aging epidermis? I'm not sure about the age of the women who represent Noxzema's prime target audience, but my common sense tells me that the vast majority have got to be over 25. But if any commercial was ever designed to turn off women who are over 25, this is the one.

I can't understand how people in the business of talking to women and selling products to them could be so insensitive to their feelings. In the long run, this commercial has got to alienate the vast majority of the product's prospects. Maybe it could have been a good commercial if they'd used a beautiful woman in her thirties who has a beautiful complexion. Then, at least, it would have been believable. As it stands now, this Noxzema commercial is laughable or cry-able, depending upon the age of the woman viewing it.

It's no way to talk to a woman.

Let's look at the subject from a different angle, because not every commercial that alienates its intended market can be called a true failure. As with Noxzema, women may actually buy the product despite weak or silly advertising.

Ad campaigns developed for Axion and Biz are two good cases in point.

I don't know exact facts and figures, but I'm sure that both Axion and Biz are huge successes, so the giant companies behind them and their advertising agencies are probably patting each other on the back congratulating themselves on their advertising genius. It's hard to argue with them, because it's always hard to argue with success, but I'm going to try, anyway.

I contend that Axion and Biz are successes *in spite of* their TV advertising. I believe they could have been even greater successes with better advertising. I believe both agencies took the easy, safe way out, reasoning that it worked before so it will work again.

In fact, it did work. Given a whole new exciting product category (namely, presoaks containing the ersatz miracle of dirt-gobbling enzymes), given astronomical advertising budgets, and given an enormous sampling program, they could scarcely have failed.

But the real point is this: Who is to say that they wouldn't have succeeded better, bigger, and, as a consequence, more lucratively, if their advertising had demonstrated a real understanding of their target audience? The thing that stands out in my mind about both brands' TV advertising is the total lack of understanding they show for today's woman. Let me give you an example.

The best Axion could come up with to sell their product was Arthur Godfrey. Not to be outdone by their competitor, and with a similar lack of inspiration, Biz came up with Eddie Albert. (Parenthetically, I fail to understand how the agency for Biz could muffle its corporate conscience long enough to mimic the competition's advertising so blatantly. Rarely have I seen two such similar commercials for two competitive products running at the same time. The respective spokesmen aside, they were virtually identical.) Let's take a close look to see whether these commercials and their spokesmen did in fact have the intended effect upon the women they were trying to sell.

First, the "tried-and-proved" technique of using a male spokesman to sell a product to women deserves a few words. This "infallible" technique was devised to capitalize on female feelings of inferiority. Women, it was felt, lack faith in themselves and would therefore lack faith in a product spokeswoman. So sponsors used this comfortable bit of reasoning to justify their use of men as the ultimate authority on any subject you could name. It worked every time for years.

This approach is highly questionable today. To say the least, women have come of age in this country. They are receiving equal education, competing quite well with men both in and out of the classroom, and are doing very well thank you in the executive job market competition. Thus, their experience with men as equals has taught them that the male of the species is *not* ominiscient. Women know a lot more than men about a lot of subjects. So one of the ways women are expressing their new-found self-confidence is in protest over the fakery they sense in men who try to be authoritative about subjects unrelated to them. Like diapers. Like dishwashing and floorwaxing. Like "feminine iron supplement requirements."

Like laundry detergent.

So open your eyes, Axion! Wake up, Biz! Why would your male spokesman be anything but totally unbelievable or laughable as he extolls the virtues of his favorite laundry soap? Are you trying to tell me that Arthur Godfrey washes his own clothes? What's Mrs. Godfrey doing in the meantime—giving the family buggy a new valve job? As a matter of fact, how would men feel watching Mary Margaret McBride telling Andy Granatelli all about motor oil and auto racing?

I don't mean to imply that today's woman can no longer be convinced by a male salesman. On the contrary, in certain product categories women distrust the opinions of other women. Take automobiles, for example. Women *will* buy an automobile from a man. Or a tire. Or an airplane. Or a TV set, a lawnmower, a stock, a paint, or a gasoline. These are all subjects women feel that men are eminently better qualified to speak about than women so far.

No one will ever be able to sell a woman romance like a man—a fragrance, a trip to an exotic island, wearing apparel, cosmetics, toiletries, and any other products a woman buys primarily with a man in mind. Sex, I'm glad to report, will be with us for a few more years, at least. It might even play a larger role in advertising than heretofore, because sex will be freer and more permissive with fewer social restraints and taboos placed upon women. So men, thank goodness, will not be out of the advertising picture, as spokesmen or anything else. (Conversely, look for more spokeswomen to be using feminine persuasion to sell men.)

But these two particular spokesmen are different people to different women. My mother, it is true, thinks Arthur Godfrey is an oracle, and she believes every word he utters. My wife knows who he is, but doesn't necessarily believe anything he says. My sister-in-law, a young woman with pre-schoolers at home, doesn't even know who he is, though his name sounds vaguely familiar to her.

Now then. My mother, the Arthur Godfrey fan, does very little washing for herself and my father. My wife does a little more with two grown children around the house occasionally. But my sister-in-law spends half her day next to the washing machine.

And she's the one who wouldn't know Arthur Godfrey from Francis X. Bushman.

To her, the only representative of the crucial 25-40 group in this sampling, Arthur Godfrey is just a kindly old man from a past generation who can't sell her a thing. He represents times gone by. He's not up-to-date to the modern homemaker. And everything she could say about Arthur Godfrey goes double for Eddie Albert. Through no fault of his own, neither of these spokesmen does his product justice. In fact, he might be doing it an injustice.

It's hard to think of these products as new, exciting innovations when they're introduced by such tired old salesmen. And the name "Biz" itself is hardly a daring new name for a product of this decade. It sounds like something left over from the thirties.

Luckily for both of these advertisers, though, the demonstration of their products' virtues, coupled with the need for the new product category they represent, put the sales message across despite their inferior vehicles.

Similarly, those silly little slice-of-life kitchen dramas that take place between two housewives debating the merits of a particular product over their breakfast coffee may be on their way out too, for the same reason. They've outworn their usefulness, though some advertisers just won't let go. They're insulting to a woman's intelligence, her femininity, and her decision-making abilities in her role as homemaker.

And speaking of being insulting to women, I'd like to say a word or two about the popular fallacy that puts daytime television forward as the most economical and efficient way to reach the non-working woman. By "non-working," of course, the media experts mean "non-employed." But you can't tell me that these "non-working" women are sitting around eating bonbons and watching TV while there's work to be done. On the contrary. The media numbers indicate that the sets are on, but that doesn't prove anyone is watching them. And even if they are being watched, the concentration probably isn't very intense, especially during the commercials. I have a hunch that busy homemakers go back to their work—or renew their work with extra energy—during the commercial breaks. Hence, although daytime TV may be the most efficient way to reach *numbers*, it doesn't necessarily reach women.

While their daytime viewing is secondary to working around the house, evening TV is probably as important to women as it is to men. Which is to say that evening is the time when they relax. Television viewing becomes the woman's primary activity, and everything else is an intrusion. To me, this says that in the evenings a woman is in a more relaxed, more receptive frame of mind for an advertiser's message. And I'd rather reach her fewer times (evening time is more expensive) when she's in that frame of mind than more often during the day.

In short, I don't care what the "Big Soapers" like Procter & Gamble and General Foods say, *I* say daytime television is no time to talk to a woman. Those heavy advertisers spend so much anyway that they can afford to waste some of their advertising dollars on daytime, just as they can afford ineffective, benign "slice-of-life" situation commercials. But I can't believe that a small advertiser can afford either. He has to outsmart, outthink, outcreate them. (Similarly, I believe that the biggies can afford to whisper their message in uninspired small space print ads; small advertisers should buy full pages.) Of course, just try and find a media expert to agree with me.

I guess the point this discussion is leading up to is this: the female consumer is changing. Rapidly, dramatically, completely, she's changing. She has been in the process of change all through the sixties. She changed more during that decade than she had changed during the previous thirty to fifty years, she's continuing to change during the seventies, and "we ain't seen nuthin' yet." She'll be changing so much so fast over the next few years that the advertising community is really going to have to hustle to keep pace.

THE change has been felt in the advertising business. More female writers and art directors and account executives (as well as product and brand managers on the client side) are already on the scene making their presence felt. You can feel it in the advertising they're turning out, and see it in the results they're getting. Not too long ago I asked a group of female ad writers for their list of the best and/or worst commercials of that particular year from the point of view of convincing a woman consumer to buy. I have great professional respect for these writers; their opinions are very different from men's, they're more gutsy and less afraid to say what they really think. Listen to what some of the brightest women in the business said about the effect of advertising on other women.

NADEEN PETERSON
● "The worst-commercial-of-the-year award goes to the commercial where a husband tells us that his wife does exercises, eats properly, gets enough rest, and takes the sponsor's product regularly. Presumably as a result, he says he 'thinks (he'll) keep her.' She is literally thrilled speechless. At the moment, I can't think whether the product is a vitamin or a laxative.

"As for the best, there were many. For spokesperson: Catherine Deneuve for Chanel. For demonstration: the thrilling Mercedes-Benz road tests. But my favorite all-around was the one featuring those beautiful kids singing that they'd like to buy the world a Coke. I believe it sold Coke and hope in equal amounts. I know the kids loved it, but it turned on my 83-year-old grandpa and my 15-month-old son as well."

FRANCINE WILVERS

● "The Ivory Liquid campaign with its 'hands' demonstration gets the booby prize. Matter of factly, it tells us that women over 30 are over the hill, washed up. We're supposed to guess which are the 'young' 20-year-old hands, and which are the 'old' 30-year-old hands. The message is clear: when you hit 30 you're through.

"The Sylvania cat and canary spot wins for me. The selling idea goes back to what television sets are all about: a clear, real-looking picture. The execution of a cat pouncing on a televised canary is a simple and dramatic demonstration."

ROZ REYNOLDS AVRETT

● "We tend to think that it's a lot easier to point the finger at the worst commercials than it is to applaud the best commercials. But maybe it isn't.

"Best? That's easy. For concept, writing, directing, production, and certainly the casting coup of the year: Catherine Deneuve for Chanel 5. Looking exquisite, sounding exquisite, she describes the part Chanel plays in her love life. So fresh and so different from the fake-sexy lines we're used to seeing and hearing for perfume and related products. There has been much speculation as to the cost of these commercials. Whatever they cost, I think they were worth it. I could almost inhale the fragrance coming out of my TV set.

FAITH POPCORN

● "Sadly, I find myself unable to extend kudos to any particular TV commercial on the basis of its creative execution, since I am appalled by the ocean of abysmal TV creative effort that we were all mistreated to this year. With an occasional exception, most of this past year's TV was barely a pipsqueak above dreadful.

"There is one TV campaign that I will, at least in one respect, toss a bouquet at—the Charmin series. I think Charmin's effort was brilliant in that its creators conceived, for a low-interest parity product, an approach that represents a legitimate first in an unfortunately look-alike, sound-alike category. Charmin conceived a remarkably new way to differentiate its product, and created a highly motivating purchase situation that no comparable package-goods product has ever even attempted before, at least to my knowledge.

"These commercials created an unusual interim condition by sandwiching, between TV exposure and the cash register experience, a tactile encounter on the part of the housewife with the product itself.

"Think of it. They combined the principles of the automotive industry's test drive with those of the free, no-obligation taste test. With most products, a woman has to plunk down her dough before she can find out if she really likes a product. In this case, Charmin got women not merely to pick the product off the shelf, but to sample its softness which, you cannot quibble, is probably the nearest thing to actual bathroom tissue product trial, at least without running the risk of arrest for indecent exposure.

"Sadly, I cannot extol this ingenious concept beyond the point of its smashingly innovative conceptual thinking. Which leads me to my nomination for the worst TV series of the year: the very same Charmin commercials. It is a pity that such a potentially bountiful idea should have been executed in a form so banal, ineloquent, tasteless, and boring. I cannot help expressing my anguished criticism, since it is my belief that, had the execution been in any way equal in brilliance to the superlative concept itself, its sales effectiveness would have been infinitely greater.

"And there were so many more imaginative executions possible! Still, Godspeed to Charmin for doing at least 50 percent of the job so well."

IF advertising people are smart, you're going to be tuning in to a whole new ball game for the next few years. Maybe advertisers won't like the idea of changing the image of women in their commercials, but they'd better pull out of their spin quickly enough to get to know their new customer. Right now, the female consumer of the future is 15 or 20 years old, and she marches to a different drummer. Advertisers who insist upon playing the same old tunes will be marching alone into oblivion.

The old rules must go. Old formulas won't work. It's a whole new exciting woman we're going to be talking to, and maybe we'll need more new exciting women in our business to talk to her. In fact, I predict that the advertising business will be dominated by women by the end of the eighties—as it should be, since they are the market advertising strives to reach. Nobody understands a woman like another woman.

We'll need more exciting men, too, but they'll have to be the right men for the right season. Goodbye Mr. Godfrey. Farewell Mr. Albert.

The king is dead. Long live the queen.

14

How Not to Talk to the Youth Market

It's probably a cliché, but it's no less true for all that: sometimes our best ideas develop from situations that come about by pure chance.

Take the "youth market" phenomenon, for example. I'd never have learned how not to talk to the youth market if a situation hadn't arisen a couple of summers ago in which I found myself with absolutely nothing to write about for my monthly column. When deadline time came close, I began a discreet search for someone who could get me off the hook. And learned something valuable as a result.

After a series of increasingly desperate phone calls to friends in the business, I finally grasped at a straw in my own office named Bill Schneider. At 23 years old, he was already a graduate of Georgetown and halfway through his sprint toward an MBA at the University of Chicago Graduate School. He was smart, serious, dedicated, committed—everything the advertising business should be attracting. Best of all, he was available, because he'd elected to spend his summer learning to write copy in my office. Not only did he jump at the chance I offered him, he left me with the distinct impression that if I hadn't asked him to contribute to my column, he would have asked me.

Bill Schneider used that column to verify some of my pet theories about the so-called youth market and to articulate a few more of his own. First of all, he cited a then-current Listerine commercial as proof that some people in advertising are really not as smart as they'd like us to believe. With its heavyhanded approach to a young audience via far too many "groovy's" and "good vibrations," the commercial puckered up for the kiss of death by trying to keep up with young people's jargon. Once these words become familiar they lose their uniqueness, and being different from the old order is something young people prize dearly.

I once wrote much the same thing in a column entitled "Selling the TV Boppers." No matter how fat their ties, how wide their bellbottoms, or how faded their jeans, I noted, the teenage "experts" at agencies are *not* teenagers. They're older, and even a few years make a difference. They work in advertising agencies, drink martinis, go to Greece and Acapulco, buy expensive clothes, dine in fancy restaurants. Any parent of a teenager knows more about teenagers than this crew does.

So what's good TV advertising to the youth market? Bill singled out the AMC Javelin commercial in which a teenager has modified his Javelin for the track and his father thinks he's butchered it. He found the commercial believable, because young people could identify with the situation, and functional, because it got the car's features across in an interesting and entertaining way.

Basically, though, Bill didn't believe in TV advertising to

young people at all. Here's what he said about the best way to reach the under-20 crowd:

> While I do think that there are a few good commercials aimed at young people, I'm also convinced that television is not the place to advertise to the youth market. The tube spews forth roughly 15 hours of mediocre programming daily. And the really beautiful thing is that today's young people are smart enough to realize that it *is* mediocre. What's more, they realize that most of the programs are irrelevant. So what impact can even a good commercial be expected to have if it's sandwiched between slices of insignificant mediocrity?
>
> Have you ever heard of a TV station whose programming is expressly aimed at young people? There's no such animal. So what's the answer?
>
> Radio. There's a growing number of radio stations that play nothing but blues, rock, folk, and acid music. Not the standard AM rock stations that play three minutes of music and ten minutes of commercials, but the new ones you'll find on FM. These stations belong to the younger generation, again because they're unique. They're something different from what the "other" generation has. And when a commercial does play, it's not immediately rejected. It's listened to, mulled over, and then accepted or rejected. What more could an advertiser ask for?

What indeed? As the father of a teenager and as an ad man, I know this audience has to be sold differently. But is radio the only medium with selling potential for this market? I tend to doubt it, though Bill made reference to a few persuasive examples of radio commercials with youth appeal taken from the Mennen Dry campaign. In one, a mother tells her daughter she can't go out in a minidress. She's all for fashion, but she doesn't want her daughter seen in public wearing nothing more than a blouse. In another, a father tells his son to wipe the dirt off his lip only to find that his son is growing a mustache. "Over my dead body, you are!" rumbles Poppa Bear. The message is simple: you're under pressure, so you need the protection of a good deodorant. The audience not only identifies with the situation; they hear it on *their* radio station, which they're already predisposed to believe.

Yes, this is a persuasive argument, but I can't help thinking that young people would respond to a good selling concept on TV as well. I know from my own experience that technique alone will not sell them; it insults them. Teenagers are in the business of asserting their authority over yours, and that makes them the toughest audience to sell. They challenge every word you say. They doubt your claims. They're defiant and rebellious. They accept nothing as fact unless you can prove it. They won't buy unless you've got a compelling reason for them to buy. They're a challenge to the ad man and we're not meeting that challenge with silly little teenage commercials.

Even though he found a great deal of TV programming to be meaningless today, Bill agreed that "television is potentially a great medium. It could be an incredibly effective means of reaching the younger generation. Maybe the answer is to have UHF TV stations, like the new FM radio stations, devoted entirely to young people." That's not a bad idea, if you're in the business of creating media. But we're in the business of creating advertising to reach an audience, and our problem is one of determining *how* to sell effectively before we take up *where* to sell effectively.

So how do you sell a teenager? Like you sell anybody else: with a good, believable selling concept that fills a need. And then please don't kill it with an execution that tries to get onto the teenage wavelength. You're not one of the gang. Teenagers resent the pretense. (Just ask Pepsi-Cola about "The Pepsi Generation." The kids laughed so hard they spilled their Cokes.) Teenagers want to be talked to like teenagers when teenagers do the talking, like adults when adults do the talking. And they know as well as we do that advertisers are adults.

How should you *not* sell the youth market? Listen to Bill Schneider; he concluded his remarks with an observation that flashes in my mind in neon letters whenever the subject arises: "Trying to be hip is a sure way to lose your audience—and your customers," he wrote. "Creating a situation which young people can identify with has the opposite effect."

Now you advertisers can get rid of all those expensive teenage "experts" on your staff and start hiring some real ad people. Like Bill Schneider.

15
How Not to Introduce a Product

In a word, don't introduce the introduction.

Oh, it's tempting. Think of all the fun the Getty Oil people must have had when they put together their "Bridge on the River Kwai" commercial to introduce a new campaign. But does "fun"—or manufactured, irrelevant excitement—transmit enough sales information to sell the product? This bit of staging didn't. All it did was to subject us to that relentless, whistling theme from the movie while scores of marching gas attendants and rolling vehicles passed in review over a bridge. It was only after the umpteenth airing that I began to discern a sales point amidst the fanfare: Getty gives you more miles for your money because Getty sells only premium quality gasoline at regular prices. Could have fooled me. I thought they were selling a brand-new sport: marching.

The irrelevant, nonfunctional, obtrusive execution actually obscured a perfectly valid sales message. The product was forgotten while the commercial marched on and on. In the interest of putting together an exciting introductory commercial, advertisers can lose their heads.

Dr. Pepper was introduced to the New York market with a commercial that totally ignored the soft drink to talk about the introduction. Worse yet, the introduction on which so much attention was lavished was in questionable (to say the least) taste.

Picture this: Nervous combat troops, in full battle gear, are smoking their last cigarettes before jumping aboard their trucks for The Big Invasion. An old, battle-hardened veteran of many campaigns is trying to calm a green, young rookie before his first big battle. It's all very realistic and grim—until the announcer informs us that "Dr. Pepper is coming to New York! Nothing can stop us now!"

What a perfectly rotten way to introduce a new product! Not only did they neglect to tell us what Dr. Pepper is or what it does; they told their young prospects, who were, at the time, organizing demonstrations to protest the Vietnam war, that they planned to invade New York City, and they used a grotesquely real, warlike scene to announce it. Brilliant, huh? That's really knowing the mood of your prospects. The result of finely-honed judgment and exquisite taste, right?

Dr. Pepper wasn't the only soft drink to make this mistake. RC Cola responded to the same challenge—introducing the product to New York—with equal stupidity. Their commercial informed us that RC Cola is not selling well in Boston, and belligerently issued an ultimatum to Boston to "Shape up or else." Some reason for New Yorkers to buy RC Cola.

When you go after competitors like Coke and Pepsi, you *must* perforce give your prospects a switching idea, a reason to try your product, or you've lost your market by default. At the very least, you must say *something* about your product.

I must admit that an introduction can say something about the product and still be bad, like the one that introduced Brim decaffeinated coffee to New York. It gave us a perfectly clear idea of what the product was all about. It just wasn't a *switching* idea, that's all.

It opens with a wife at the breakfast table forbidding her husband to have another cup of coffee and sadistically rationing his share to half a cup. This, so he can sleep at night. (I'd lose sleep if I had a wife like that, too.)

In the next scene, we find her crowing over her new discovery: Brim, tasting as good as his favorite brand, but decaffeinated to let him sleep.

Where have we heard that strategy before? Merely in every other decaffeinated coffee commercial on the air. Sanka has done the same thing for years, and better, with their "hidden camera" approach. So why shouldn't I stick with Sanka? Give me one reason, Brim—*any* reason—to switch.

As an introductory commercial, this one left something to be desired. Like excitement, news, and believability.

Why can't there be more introductory commercials like the one that told the world about Alka-Seltzer Cold Tablets? It began with a standard announcer's pitch for the new product. Then, suddenly, an off-screen voice began lobbing questions at the announcer. Both the questions and the answers covered everything we need to know before we'd buy the product. The commercial ended with the voice asking if this is a real, live commercial.

And there it is. Four important points were made (the introduction, the nature of the product, why we need it, and the maker of the product) in a refreshingly irreverent way that didn't distract us from the concept.

That's what an introduction should do.

Unless advertisers draw attention to the product itself and its Unique Advantage, their efforts are doomed to only partial (at best) success.

Save the fanfare.

Sell the product, not the introduction.

16
How Not to Sell a Car

RIGHT AFTER VIDEO TEST PATTERNS AND "CELEBRITY Bowling," automotive commercials were my least favorite TV fare until a few years ago. Remember Petula Clark singing "The Beat Goes On" for Plymouth? No sales points were made about the car, no demonstration of the automobile's solid merits distracted our attention from the attractively angled photography, but the undefined "beat" went on. And on. And on. At approximately the same time, Pontiac was seriously suggesting that "Wide-Tracking" would replace boating, fishing, baseball, football, tennis, golf, and possibly sex as the number one leisure activity in the country, and Oldsmobile trumpeted apologies for its name by introducing Youngmobiles (blah!) to a new generation. During those Dark Ages, a great plaque known as Dodge Fever (possibly the terminal stage of Dodge Rebellion) swept the land, subjecting us to an epidemic of commercials starring that year's blonde instead of the previous year's brunette.

Looking back on this era, I marvel that any of these commercials were actually produced and aired. It seems as if Detroit kept its eyes and ears tightly shut so as not to become contaminated by what was happening in advertising all around them. Maybe that's why all of their commercials looked 25 years old conceptually. It was almost a shock to see brand new cars in them. Those were the days when gaudy, glittering Hollywood techniques were meant to disguise the anemic effort that went into "Thinking Young," when a shrill appeal to eyes and emotions was thought to be more "with it" than a lucid appeal to reason or the mind.

In those days I used my *Madison Avenue* column to hurl one smoking indictment after another at the agencies and corporations who supported the whole sorry mess. "There's no more competitive business than the automobile business," I fumed in one column, "and it's about time Detroit stopped treating the car-buying public like a bunch of kids being offered shiny new toys, and started talking to them like the sophisticated consumers they are. It's about time someone admitted that there is competition in the auto business. It's about time someone tried to show us why he makes a better product than his competitor. It's about time someone gave us good reasons why we should buy his car. Wake up, Detroit! We're big boys and girls now!"

Then, suddenly, something happened to automotive advertising: it got better. Not from any burst of aesthetic integrity, mind you, but purely because of the influx of foreign cars from Germany, France, Italy, Sweden, England, and Japan. Car makers from these countries brought more than chrome and metal with them. They brought facts and figures so they could talk sense to the American people. We listened so carefully that Detroit began to get frightened. And rightfully so.

Instead of showing fashion models tooling around circular driveways to their half-a-million-dollar mansions, the foreign car manufacturers talked about double-disc brakes, overhead cams, safety features, price, gas mileage, and 11-year life spans. While hundreds of chrome-dipped monsters with childish names revolved on pedestals at the annual orgies we call Automobile Shows, the foreign car manufacturers used their ads to take potshots at the whole American concept of planned obsolescence, new models annually, and yards of chrome trim.

Commercials for foreign cars were executed in a style to which we were definitely not accustomed. No cast-of-thousands extravaganzas. No cars perched atop mountain peaks. No bathing beauties. No Ringling Brothers special effects. Their commercials were simple, direct, inexpensive. The car became the hero in place of the scenario, and the audience bought it. In droves.

Bit by bit, Detroit responded to the transportation wants of the nation by introducing smaller, more economical, and less ostentatious automobiles, but you still wondered if they were watching the same TV channels as the rest of us. As their cars became simpler and more economical, their commercials drove hell-for-leather in the opposite direction. Hollywood had come to stay in Detroit. They tried humor. They tried jingles. The prospects laughed and sang along with American car commercials, but since these commercials didn't invite them to actually *buy* anything, they didn't. The laughter and singing became giggles and humming and then stopped altogether.

There was a lot of head scratching on Detroit's West Grand Boulevard.

Meanwhile, back at the cash register, the foreign car manufacturers were pitchforking their profits back into more TV commercials, and what beauties they were! The Volkswagen series comes to mind first, of course, because they never seemed to run out of fresh ideas. In a nutshell, the genius of their advertising was its ability to overcome the unique disadvantage inherent in the look of the car by drawing attention to VW's many other unique advantages. At the same time, those commercials turned the distinctive VW look into a reverse-snob-appeal advantage.

Their tools were simplicity, believability, honesty, and conviction. My all-time favorite was the "Keeping up with the Kremplers" spot in which a short story unfolds about two next-door neighbors, Mr. Jones and Mr. Krempler. As the scene begins, Mr. Jones is parking his new car in the driveway of his home. Next door, an army of deliverymen carries a refrigerator, a range, a dishwasher, two television sets, a hi-fi, and a whole truckload of other goodies into Mr. Krempler's house. Dumbfounded, Mr. Jones's frustration is complete when Krempler himself pulls up at the rear of the procession driving a spanking new Volkswagen, and the point is made that he was able to buy all those things with just the difference in price between his VW and Mr. Jones's new car. It ends on a line that asks how the Joneses will ever be able to keep up with the Kremplers. A great concept, a great execution.

Another commercial in the same campaign made a similar point by featuring an Arab oil potentate who didn't need a VW because he's got plenty of oil, gas, and moola. However ironic this one may seem since the oil embargo, its sales point is stronger than ever.

To illustrate the breadth of VW's product line, another commercial introduced Harry the Swinger, who starts out as a bachelor Karmann Ghia owner. Then he marries and keeps buying bigger and bigger Volkswagens to keep up with his growing family and in-laws. Finally he gives up and leaves his family. Single once more, he buys a "swinging" Karmann Ghia sports car for himself, again. A clever way, I thought, to show what a great family car the Volkswagen is, with different sizes available for different sized families.

Finally, there was a commercial designed to show us how Volkswagen is constantly improving its product without resorting to the planned obsolescence strategy of its American competitors. It's shot in black and white, set and propped to evoke memories of the old $64,000-question quiz show. When contestant Gino is asked the jackpot question ("How many changes have been made in the brand-new Volkswagen?") he answers "None"—and loses his chance to win a fortune. Volkswagen makes hundreds of changes to make the car run better, the voice-over explains smoothly, but few that you can see.

With advertising help like this, how could VW fail to capture a healthy segment of the automotive market? Oh, I don't mean to say that they never made a mistake—they made lots of them. Sometimes their famous understatement was so "under" that the statement skyrocketed right over our heads. Take VW's "There is no killing the Beetle" commercials for example. An animated cartoon, it showed a little VW driving all over the TV screen. Suddenly, everyone's trying to kill the poor little beetle, first by squashing it with a giant thumb, then by swatting it with a fly swatter. Asphyxiation via a huge can of insect repellent follows and a giant foot tries to grind it into the ground to the accompaniment of fiendish laughter. But nothing can stop the beetle. After each attack, it picks itself up and keeps going.

This commercial is a loser because it fails to tell us *who* is trying to kill the beetle, *why* they're trying to rub it out, and *what difference it would make* if they succeeded. It makes no point. Gives not one clear reason for anyone to buy the car. And if they were trying to make a point about the indestructibility of the VW, they missed, because their allegory-cum-fantasy situations were too far removed from reality to be understood or believed. If you'll pardon the pun, the commercial was 100 percent execution. Whatever basic concept lurked at the heart of it was obscured by technical overkill.

I remember another commercial in which a flock of penguins represented people in full-dress suits. With the noise of traffic in the background, they mill around, multiply in number, walk toward several Volkswagens and mingle among the cars. "On a hot and humid night," purrs the announcer, "when you're dressed up to go out with friends, we just want you to know that Volkswagens can now be equipped with air conditioning."

Well, it isn't as bad as the "Can't kill the Beetle" spot because at least it makes a clear point. But however significant the message, it's so subservient to the execution that it's all but lost. It seems to me that the least memorable part of this commercial is the air-conditioning message, a line seemingly tacked on as an afterthought. Up until that point, they were selling penguins.

Then there was the VW commercial that unsold the product.

Yes, I said unsold, and the victim was Karmann Ghia. To parody a typical car commercial demonstration, they showed a number of sports cars breaking through canvas barriers. When its turn comes, the Karmann Ghia is unable to break through. The audio says, "Karmann Ghia is the most economical sports car you can buy, it's just not the most powerful." Believe it or not, that's the commercial.

In strict fairness, I have to admit that this commercial is

simple, believable, and convincing. Unfortunately, in this case every one of those noble ingredients works to the disadvantage of the product. Why be honest to the point of absurdity? It seems to me that the authors of this one went well beyond the call of duty to find a disadvantage, then blew it way out of proportion for the sake of a gag. They got their gag, all right, but in the process they unforgivably damaged the product's image. You couldn't get me to buy a Karmann Ghia after that. All the good feelings I had about the car were reversed. Maybe that's one of the reasons the car is no longer made. Who wants a sports car with all the thrust of a flea? And would you believe it—this commercial won The Copy Club's coveted Gold Key award that year. *I* believe it. That's why I've always been so against all this award nonsense in advertising.

Sales should be a commercial's only award.

The same kind of superior advertising that built an empire for the small and very ugly little VW produced similar results for Volvo. If any one commercial could be said to typify Volvo's consistently good advertising effort, it would have to be the one that opened with a Volvo driving along a highway past abandoned American cars. The audio gives the 11-year story, a powerful, believable, single-minded point they have driven home since the beginning of their advertising in the United States. It is simply this: Volvos last an average of 11 years in Sweden where the roads are not paved, so no one knows how long they might last here. Then the announcer delivers the coup de grace: "Other cars may last 11 years (pause), but they're not driving." This, as the Volvo passes scrapped car after scrapped car along the roadside. The commercial ends with these words appearing on the screen: "Volvo lives."

No fun. No games. No jokes. No jingles. Just plain,

simple, solid, believable sell. Someone who is about to involuntarily junk a car that cost him three to five thou a short three or four years ago can be counted on to feel a definite twinge watching this commercial. This was a great concept, and the stark, dramatic realism of its execution packs a terrific wallop.

Another great Volvo commercial was the "House-Eating Monster" cartoon that featured a car in the garage which turns into a monster and eats its owner out of house and home. It was brilliant. One I didn't particularly like was called "Lars of Arabia." The point the "Lars" commercial made with a sheik driving across the desert to a Volvo test station, is that Volvos are made to stand up under any weather conditions, tropical or arctic. I found it ho-hum, forced, and not terribly original. Even so, Volvo's advertising has been consistently excellent over the years.

Datsun has done some fine TV work as well. Two examples spring to mind: in one, a spokesman delivers his message to us while standing in the middle of a drenched highway. He is talking about Datsun's brakes and how they hold even when they get wet. Far off in the background, we see a car racing toward the announcer. He keeps talking calmly as the car splashes closer and closer through puddle after puddle until it is about to mow him down. At the last moment, the brakes are applied firmly and the Datsun screeches to a stop not more than inches from the announcer's rear. Unfazed and unflustered, the announcer brings his spiel to a smooth ending by stressing the importance of well-functioning brakes. They sure were important to him, he concludes, or he wouldn't be here.

To repeat, there's nothing as dramatic as a demonstration where someone stakes his life on the product's ability to perform as advertised. You can't beat that for believability.

The other Datsun spot is easily the most unusual automobile commercial I've ever seen. It's the true story of an
ex-millionaire (he is real, and is identified). We follow him as
he strolls along the streets of his town and tells us his story
of his meteoric rise in business—and his sudden fall. According to him, he used to own a Rolls-Royce and he loved
it, but when he lost everything, including the Rolls, he
replaced it with a Datsun. Indicating the car, parked in
front of his now-modest home, he says "It's no Rolls-Royce,
but it's a great car," and he vows he'll keep it even after he
hits the top again and buys another Rolls. It's all done so
simply, so humanly, and so honestly that I came away believing every word he said about the Datsun. He never said
the Datsun compares in any way to the Rolls, because that
would have been ludicrous. He merely gives the impression
that, for the money, it's a heck of a car. And although you
get hooked on the story of the man's personal affairs, it never
gets in the way of the selling of the car. On the contrary, the
story adds interest and believability to the sales pitch.

In an entirely different way, Mercedes commercials make
me feel like standing up and cheering. Mercedes makes
commercials the same way they make cars: precise, efficient,
direct, unemotional. There is absolutely no borrowed interest in any of their commercials; it's 100 percent about the
product, and nothing is allowed to interfere, not even an
actor. There's only one star, and that's the car. Take the
spot in which six Mercedes perform a routine on the test
track, a sensational demo of the automobile's precision handling and maneuverability. The routine itself is exciting to
watch and fraught with suspense, while the audio makes the
point that Mercedes-Benz is so precision-engineered that the
six cars perform as one. Along the way, points are made
about the car's disc brakes, steering, and so on. It adds up to

a commercial that's as exciting to watch as it is instructive. Good for us and good for Mercedes.

Talking about strong commercials, how about the one that not only had the chutzpah to tackle Mercedes, the aristocrat of automobiles, but actually scored a few, meaningful points against it? That's just what Mazda did in one of the most sensational automotive commercials of 1973 by zeroing in on the one point of comparison in which Mazda has the clear edge—pick-up speed.

The Mazda and Mercedes line up on a starting line. The announcer tells us that both cars are capable of doing 120 miles per hour, but in a quarter-mile race from a standing start, the lighter, rotary-engined Mazda wins, and we *see* it win convincingly. Rubbing salt in Mercedes' wounds, the commercial goes on to point out that for the price of the losing Mercedes, you can buy this Mazda . . . and this one . . . and this one.

A great commercial . . . a great commercial . . . a great commercial.

How did spots like these go over in Detroit? For one thing, the head scratching stopped. For another, the eyes were opened. And finally, the gears started turning. Slowly, but they were turning. Before long, American cars—not all of them, but enough to be encouraging—were being sold via effective, no-nonsense commercials, too.

The first sign of a breakthrough was Ford's "Quiet ride" campaign, an approach that succeeded for several reasons. First, their positioning was unique—nobody else was talking about a quiet ride. Second, the "quiet factor" is an important element in a car-buying decision, particularly for Ford because of Ford's old but not forgotten reputation for producing rattle-ridden tin lizzies. Third, a "quiet ride" is demonstrable, and they did it well.

The earliest "quiet" commercials featured the car's window opening and closing in the middle of a noisy outside environment. But this demo, while good, failed to get to the guts of Ford's rattling problem. Nor was it unique, since all cars become quieter inside when their windows are closed. Ford hit the believability jackpot when they produced a commercial that stars an audiometer measuring the sound level inside their car (65 decibels) as it rides along a smooth-surfaced road. Suddenly, the car is subjected to a shake/torture test so strenuous that the gas tank must be removed and the shocks cooled to avoid overheating. That was the windup; now comes the pitch.

Pretorture test conditions are duplicated—the smooth road, the steady speed—and the audiometer is put to work again to see if any parts have become loose and noisy. They haven't. The audiometer registers the same 65 decibles as before, and Ford proves that it builds automobiles that stay tight and quiet under stress.

Even better than the "quiet ride" was the "Ford has a better idea" campaign that followed, and recently they topped that with a commercial that struck me as one of the simplest, most unusual, most effective commercials possible for any product. It never showed a car and it didn't talk about features. It didn't even try to sell me anything. But oh, what a selling job it did for Ford!

Quite simply, the commercial posed three true-or-false questions to potential car buyers. They all sounded true to me, but then an announcer informed me that they were all false. "Today," he continued, "you have to know more about cars before you buy one, so please write in for a free Ford booklet called 'Car Buying Made Easier.' The first part of the booklet is completely devoted to automotive facts, and the last part is prejudiced—it's all about Ford products."

This commercial is more institutional than product-oriented, so it's probably unfair to compare it with most of the hard-sell commercials Ford runs, but considering that a good many car purchasers are more influenced by the name of the manufacturer than by the model itself, this is one of the hardest-selling commercials Ford has ever run. If you're in the market for a new car—any car—you've *got* to write away for that booklet. It's a refreshing, honest, and provocative low-key commercial, and I got the nice feeling from it that Ford really cares. And that's quite a change from the typical "Detroit" commercials that Ford used to run.

Like the one that featured a henpecked man who asserts himself by pushing over a Ford dealer (actually a 5-foot punching bag that keeps popping back up). Having proved himself on the Ford dealer, henpecked husband then works up the courage to stand up to his domineering wife. Was the point that Ford dealers are pushovers? or that they take a lot of punishment? Neither one is the kind of image I'd like to cultivate if I were a Ford dealer. Moreover, I'd never, never buy a car from such a spineless fool, nor would I trust him to make good on my warranty. A quiet ride and a free booklet are *much* more attractive.

I'm obliged to mention, however, that in hot pursuit of a sales point, more than one American car manufacturer emerged with a slightly bedraggled image. At least in the early stages of the game, before American car commercials drew abreast of their foreign competitors. Take Chrysler. I have no quarrel with what they actually said in their first series of no-nonsense commercials; information about unibody construction, rust prevention, and life span was precisely what the public thirsted for after the situation comedies and irritating jingles of the previous decade. It's just that I wonder if you can guess the name of the spokesman who delivered their message about their new, modern technology. Ready? Your three seconds are up! It's . . .

Arthur Godfrey again.

Now see here. Arthur Godfrey has been the greatest electronic-medium salesman of all time, and for some products, I'm sure he'd still be a convincing spokesman. Life insurance, maybe. A retirement village, an airline, a resort, golf clubs, or fishing gear. But definitely *not* a Chrysler automobile when Chrysler's image already connotes everything square and establishment. Why do they pick a spokesman who epitomizes everything establishment, thereby fortifying the image and compounding the problem? Listening to Arthur Godfrey as he punctuates each sales point with a line about "the kind of car America wants," I have to ask myself how does Arthur Godfrey know what kind of car America wants? He doesn't relate to the younger generations, who represent the big car-buying market. If Chrysler's strategy was to get through to young people, they could have saved their money. It didn't work. They failed to convince this market that Chrysler builds stylish, exciting young cars. It's not Arthur Godfrey's fault, it's the agency's fault for the miscasting goof of the year.

In TV advertising, above all other media, it's not just what you say and how you say it that count, it's also who says it for you and Arthur Godfrey is not the man to say it for Chrysler. The car's image just can't take it.

Nor can Buick afford the monumental mistake made by the Tri-State (New York, New Jersey, and Connecticut) Buick Dealers not so long ago. They launched an extensive campaign with the overall theme "If you'll price a Buick, you'll buy a Buick." I recall three well-executed commercials in this series; the first featured a jackhammer operator, the second a Central Park hansom cab driver, and the third a toll collector. The idea behind these commercials is that each of these workers can afford a Buick. The problem the Buick dealers thought they were solving is obvious: A survey was probably conducted proving that the lower middle class considers Buick to be a high-priced car beyond their economic reach. Hence these three commercials to show blue-collar workers, who are buying the middle and top end of the low-priced car lines, how affordable a Buick is.

The marketing strategy is sound. But I'm amazed that such ignorance of the psychological factors affecting a car-buying decision could exist at the crucial retail level. To many, a car is not only a means of physical transportation; it signifies psychological transportation as well. To recognition, to pride, to status. A car fortifies our personal image, and its purchase is never taken lightly. This is especially true of the lower-to-middle income group that is the target audience of this campaign, because although they can never compete with the affluent for homes grand enough to serve as status symbols, they *can* compete, thanks to relatively lenient auto financing, for almost any automobile. If they can't swing a new one, they can certainly afford a second-hand car with almost the same first-class status. This is what accounts for the tremendous popularity of luxury cars on the resale market.

A man's home may be his castle, but his car is his kingdom.

That being the case, who the hell wants to drive the same car that a jackhammer operator drives, especially if we happen to be jackhammer operators ourselves? The class is gone. The prestige is gone. The status is gone. The very reasons these people would want a Buick in the first place. It's just human nature to want to better yourself, and that means reaching for a stratum above, not below yourself.

How could the Tri-State Buick Dealers be so ignorant of anything so important and so obvious? Any good car salesman could have told them about that! In the end, they managed to drag their product's image down with the economy message, an object lesson in how *not* to sell a car.

On the other hand, I hope Mercury has been selling lots of cars with their new demo; they've done some excellent ones since the day they realized that show biz doesn't sell automobiles. Like Ford's quiet ride, Mercury's Montego sells its smooth ride, a strong demonstrable point they've driven home with such single-minded energy that it's begun to assume folkloric proportions. In the early stages of the campaign, commercials featured a wine tasting, then a little girl practicing her penmanship, and finally a diamond cutter splitting a valuable gem—each while riding along a bumpy road in a Montego. One particularly fine spot showed a Montego and a herd of galloping horses speeding side by side along a stretch of rough terrain. While a wheel-mounted camera films the horses from outside the car, a photographer-passenger films the same scene from the interior of the car. When the two strips of film are compared on a split screen, the exterior footage is jumpy and rough and the scene filmed from inside is smooth and even—thanks to Montego's superior suspension.

The best commercials in this series used a plain old tried-and-true blindfold test, the kind you never see in car commercials. Several people, named and identified, are blindfolded and taken on three test rides, the first in a Mercury, the second in a $16,000 limousine, and the third in a $26,000 European touring car. When asked which car gave them the smoothest, quietest, most luxurious ride, the overwhelming majority of the participants chose the Mercury—before the identities of the three cars were revealed. In this, as in others of the same series, success was the result of a valid selling point treated to a simple, convincing demonstration. Nothing sells like a good demo.

Just ask American Motors about that.

In the bad old days, when Detroit's "sporty" cars battled the foreign invaders for the small car market, AMC put three blockbuster commercials on the air that paved the way for their ultimate victory. Not a small part of that battle was cutting out the *other* American sporty cars first, before taking on the imports. Javelin was American Motors' answer to the Mustang, and in one 60-second spot, they really took off the gloves and sold the Javelin feature for feature against the Ford Mustang. When they got done, it was convincing enough to slow any Mustang prospect's gallop toward the Ford corral—the ultimate end of any comparison commercial. All it showed was a wrecking crew taking apart a car we were led to believe was a Mustang, then putting together a better one with better parts at a lower price. That's the Javelin. And it's sold with one of the simplest, strongest commercials I've ever seen anywhere.

Another early AMC demo sold free air conditioning in their Ambassador. Six big men get into a showroom model on a hot summer day to enjoy their lunch in the pleasant, air-conditioned atmosphere of the Ambassador. While the size of the car is demonstrated visually, the audio concentrates on the freebie air-conditioner, a welcome message to anyone who's ever shelled out $200 to $300 for an air-conditioning option.

With a similar execution, a Rebel commercial featured a group of American Motors workmen, each of whom demonstrates a single feature of the car that is unique to its size and class. It adds up to a lot of unique features, and a lot of good reasons to buy the car. But then they got overconfident. One of the worst automotive commercials I've seen showed one Rebel owner asking his neighbor, another Rebel owner, how he likes the sunroof on his new car. From there on, everything is chaos. For an appalling few seconds, the beefy, obnoxious neighbor sticks his head through the sunroof, braying horrible poetry about the sun in the morning and the stars at night until, in a shrill crescendo of hopelessly mixed metaphors, he slides back into his seat and asks if that answers the question.

No, dammit, it does not.

This is just an example of how an exaggerated execution can overpower a simple selling point. Rebel is now offering a sunroof. A seemingly easy point to make, yes? Then why muck it up with so distasteful, so contrived, so stupid an execution? Obviously, it isn't even a very effective one, since I later learned that the sunroof is offered *free* as standard equipment, a point utterly obscured by the sun, the stars, and the poetry. Imagine! The most important point of the commercial—a free sunroof—was so overpowered by a nonsensical execution that it utterly failed to get through.

But then, that's show biz again.

Much as I love one, a strong, unvarnished demo isn't the only way to sell a car. American Motors sold (and is selling) a whole lot of them with a campaign so unusual it may even eclipse the foreign car commercials.

I'm talking about the American Motors Buyer Protection Plan. It's a perfectly legitimate way to sell cars. Just offer the people something extra—like this unique guarantee, for instance—and promote it as heavily as possible. If the plan is anywhere near as good as the promotion, AMC is in clover.

There's a commercial in this campaign that's really a knockout, the introductory one that describes the plan and the way it affects all brand-new American Motors cars. Briefly stated, their new cars are guaranteed for 12 months or 12,000 miles for *labor* as well as parts. When you consider that no one and no warranty has ever guaranteed the cost of labor before, you've got to admit that it's a pretty attractive deal. All you have to do, if the car breaks down through some fault of theirs, is to bring it back to them. They'll fix it. Free. *And* they'll give you a loaner to drive if the repair is going to take longer than one day. The commercial itself is simple and to the point, delivered (appropriately enough) by an American Motors mechanic. No frills, no poetry. Just 100 percent solid sell.

To reinforce the point, another AMC commercial demonstrates how few parts are covered by their competitors' warranties in comparison to the number covered by their own Buyer Protection Plan. Imagine a chart like this one: In a column stretching from the top to the bottom of the left-hand side of your TV screen, the major, competing automobiles are listed: AMC, Ford, Chevrolet, Chrysler, and so on. In a horizontal line across the very *top* of your screen, all the auto parts that could possibly be warrantied by an auto company are listed in a single line . . . transmission, electrical system, air conditioning, brakes, et cetera. Suddenly, "yes" or "no" lights begin to pop on all along the columns to indicate which auto parts are covered by which manufacturers. Reading down the line for Plymouth, for example, you might see all no's except for one yes. The same for Ford. Here's a clear indication that the competitors warrant almost none of these parts on their new cars. Midway through the commercial, you begin to get the point: the AMC line is lit up like a Christmas tree with straight yesses—positive proof of the superiority of the AMC Buyer Protection Plan.

I love this commercial! First because it sells the product. Second, because it demonstrates the very point I've been trying to make about advertising for years: the more competitive the commercial, the stronger its sales message. Name calling is not a sin if the point to be made is valid.

And as an extension of their Buyer Protection Plan commercials, a spot for Gremlin ties together the selling of a particular AMC model and the plan. It stresses the point that other car manufacturers road test only one out of every 50 cars. Gremlin tests *every* car. From there, it's only a step to the Buyer Protection Plan, and the clincher is delivered with considerable momentum: AMC takes more trouble in making the Gremlin so it will cause less trouble once you get it. The care taken in the manufacturing and the guarantee dovetail so perfectly that I doubt if the most rabid of the big three car fans could fail to be sold, or, at the very least, impressed.

I like this campaign. It's based on solid advantages for the consumer, it's simple, and it's believable. As a campaign it won't garner as many awards as some of the previous AMC campaigns—like the show-stopping "Driving Lesson" spot that illustrates a sales point of dubious value (*More driving schools use AMC Rebels than any other car*) with a superb piece of comedy, using a hapless female driving student as the butt of the jokes. As a matter of fact, the car and the message were completely secondary and incidental to the comedy (it could have been any car), but the award committees loved the commercial anyway for its really funny, well-timed, exquisitely directed and performed highjinks of the variety that detract utterly from the sales message. In this case it didn't matter because there *was* no sales message. It knocked 'em dead at the awards dinners—but I'm willing to bet that in the long run, any of the Buyer Protection Plan commercials will knock this one dead in the show rooms.

And in the last analysis that's what counts: selling more cars. When it's honest, like AMC commercials, simple like the Mercedes campaign, clever like Volkswagen's ads, or strong like Mercury's and Ford's, the commercial sells the car. That's what Detroit forgot until the straight-talking imports taught them a new lesson in competition.

17
The Cardinal Sin of Advertising

SOME ADVERTISING PRACTITIONERS WILL LOOK YOU RIGHT in the eye and tell you that the single worst fate a commercial can suffer is death by neglect. Proponents of this position insist that they would rather have their commercial noticed and hated than ignored. To them, it's better to have the product name registered negatively than not registered at all. This is the old "spit-on-the-table" George Washington Hill school of advertising.

(To all of you not old enough to have seen *The Hucksters*, a movie based on a novel about advertising, by Frederic Wakeman, starring Clark Gable as the good guy—ad agency man, of course—here is the background for that label. There is a scene in the film where the mean, old client spits on a conference-room table to the utter amazement and disgust of the assembled executives. He then makes his point that they didn't like what he did, but none of them would ever forget it. That, he remarks, is what he expects of his advertising. The scene and the character were rumored to be based on the legendary George Washington Hill, Chairman, President, Marketing Director, Advertising Director, and everything else at The American Tobacco Company at the time, who had the reputation of being the world's toughest client. This kind of advertising became known as the George Washington Hill school).

I couldn't disagree with it more. While they may be right in saying that being ignored is the worst indignity *advertising* can suffer, it is infinitely preferable to the worst indignity an *advertiser* can suffer: that of watching the public turn against his product. For the public to ignore his advertising is one thing; to be revolted by it is plainly another.

In short, bad advertising is curable. Bad taste can be fatal.

I have seen (and so have you) thousands of bad commercials. They're a dime a dozen. But happily, we don't see too many commercials in genuine bad taste any more, a fact that makes the occasional klinker all the harder to swallow. If you see three such klinkers in a single month, as I did not so long ago, you begin to get the trembles about the future of the advertising business, and a whole *rash* of them confirms this feeling. The bad taste syndrome must eventually hurt the client as well as outrage the public, and it can do irreparable damage to the entire advertising business. That's what makes it so dangerous.

This is what I mean by bad taste.

Dr. Scholl has been promoting his foot odor antiperspirant spray with the same old theme that every soap, deodorant, toothpaste, and mouthwash has used at least once: "You may be the last to know. . . ." The commercial is divided into the familiar three-scene format. (The three-scene format has become quite common in 30-second commercials. To build suspense and interest in the commercial, three vignettes are used to dramatize and drive home the same point. One scene would stretch out too long for the time span and be dull. Two scenes aren't convincing or memorable enough. Three scenes seem to be just right to make the point, add interest, and fit perfectly into the alloted time.) In the first, a man removes his shoe and hands it to a shoemaker for repairs. The shoemaker passes out. The second scene takes place in a bowling alley: one of the bowlers on a team takes off his shoes to change into his bowling shoes and his three teammates faint dead away. Predictably, when a man removes his shoe in the third scene, his dog topples over.

Come on now, Dr. Scholl. When dealing with so personal a problem and product, shouldn't you have bent over backwards *not* to be insulting? This commercial goes out of its way to do just the opposite. It's insulting to the very people who are the product's prime prospects—those who are aware of the problem and re embarrassed by it!

Wouldn't Scholl have bee1 better off handling the problem seriously by offering the delicate reassurance to "sufferers" that their problem is quite common and can now be easily eliminated? And wouldn't it have been more compatible with their theme ("You may have it without knowing it") to have directed their message to the far larger market that may not even be aware of the problem? Instead, Scholl chose to dramatize people with such obviously severe cases that, unless their nasal passages have been blocked with portland cement, they've *got* to know.

Something else about this commercial irks me: Why is the problem limited to men only? Don't women, particularly those who wear boots all day, have the same problem? (Now there's a marketing segmentation idea: a foot deodorant specifically made for a woman's special foot odor problem.) And just look at the people they chose to be the offended parties . . . . who cares about offending a shoemaker, a bowling team, or a dog? The shoemaker, let's face it, must regard foot odor as an occupational hazard, the bowlers couldn't care less, and the dog likes to lick feet anyway.

The people we are most concerned about offending are those with whom we have some significant social contact. A wife, for example, or a girlfriend. Neighbors, associates, clients. One's peers. My point is that this commercial, besides being needlessly insulting, is downright dumb.

Or, for pure nausea, how about the Safeguard soap commercial in which Daughter comes home from a date in tears because her boyfriend has given her a bar of Safeguard as a subtle hint. Her father becomes incensed, storms outside to rake the boyfriend over hot coals for implying that his little girl has body odor, and returns a minute later saying, "The boy makes a lot of sense." Daddy bursts into tears. Mother bursts into tears. Daughter is already weeping buckets, so the whole family joins together for a cozy sobbing session.

This is advertising? I can't imagine a more tasteless, insulting, repulsive way to sell a deodorant soap. There's a complete lack of sensitivity and tact and human feeling. I think it's a crying shame.

Second only to personal hygiene commercials, the most offensive ads are the ones that misuse religious characters. A case in point is a Dodge Colt commercial that features two priests (actors, of course) to deliver the sales message. They are an obvious takeoff on the Barry Fitzgerald/Bing Crosby team that sold so many tickets to *The Bells of St. Mary's*. The young priest shows the older priest the new car he has bought for the church to offer as first prize in the church raffle. He then makes all the sales points about the car's luxury features, and when he tells the old priest the price, the older man (in his thickest Barry Fitzgerald brogue and over-the-top-of-his glasses twinkle) declares that there's really no need for the parish to know how inexpensive the car really is.

In other words, let's pull a fast one on the parish.

Depicting men of the cloth in a commercial is always risky, and forcing the priest to make the actual sales pitch is even more questionable. But implying that they would even entertain the thought of deceiving the parish is highly improper, and I've got to believe that a large segment of the people who saw it (and not just the churchgoers, either) were offended and were left with a negative impression of Dodge. Was it worth it?

Another kind of bad-taste commercial is the kind that tries to frighten its audience into buying the product. A Metropolitan Life spot of not too long ago made this mistake. An animated commercial, it shows an angel having a conversation with another angel who happens to be his insurance agent. Angel 1 is kicking himself all over heaven for not having taken out insurance for his family while he was still alive. Angel 2 isn't offering him much comfort with his constantly repeated "I told you so's" (Why agent/angel is also dead is never explained, though I suspect he was probably murdered by a disgruntled client after his third "I told you so."), and the commercial ends with hapless Angel 1 uttering this deathless epitaph: "One bad mistake and you hear about it forever." This, my dearly beloved friends, is a commercial in awful taste.

I richly resent an insurance company that (1) plays on my love for my family, (2) tries to make me feel guilty, and (3) scares the hell out of me. The implication is, of course, that if I don't buy their insurance I am a terrible father and a thoughtless husband. What's more, I can look forward to an eternity in a heaven that's as bad as purgatory for my oversight, plagued by the MetLife angel in the hereafter and by my fears for my family in the here and now. Damnation!

Selling through fear went out with the Middle Ages. If Metropolitan Life thinks that their lighthearted handling of death takes the curse off this terrible commercial, they're wrong. If anything, it makes me all the more resentful and angry. It appalls me, because the decision to buy or not to buy insurance is a considered one, and no matter what a glib insurance agent tells you, it's expensive. Planning an estate, whether it includes life insurance or not, takes considerable thought and guidance by trusted counsel. *That's* what Met-Life should be telling me instead of trying to scare me into purchasing more coverage. If the viewer already feels guilty for not having enough insurance (and maybe he can't afford it), why make him feel worse? It won't make him buy more insurance. And if he doesn't feel guilty, a commercial that plays upon guilt and fear is wasted. Finally, if by some quirk the commercial manages to convince some viewers that they should have some life insurance, why should they buy a policy from Metropolitan Life? Is their insurance better? Who knows? Because all this commercial attempts to do is to sell life insurance, not Metropolitan life insurance. So what's the point?

Just this: Advertisers should never commit the bad taste error of trying to scare people into buying their products. Convince them? Yes. Reason with them? Of course. Debate them? Always. But scare them, never. MetLife angel notwithstanding, they'll tell the advertiser to go to hell.

Among the worst and most offensive commercials I've seen, though, were the ones from Colgate's "Some families have it and some don't" campaign. You have to work pretty hard to make a toothpaste commercial morally offensive, so Colgate's agency must have *slaved* over this one.

There were several executions of the same theme, each of which always contrasted two families. One family is handsome, all-American, immaculate, Aryan looking, and simply unable to do anything wrong. The other family is invariably swarthy, loutish, stupid, clumsy, sloppy, and incapable of doing anything right. The all-American family, for example, catches all the fish, but the others can't catch a one. The Good Guys are model campers while the Bad Guys are bungling idiots. The Good Guys fly a kite like NASA technicians, but the Bad Guys can't get it off the ground. The Good Guys, of course, use Colgate toothpaste, to give themselves the double ring of confidence—fluoride confidence plus mouthwash confidence—while the nebbishes (by implication) couldn't achieve similar results with Borax.

The first time I ever saw this commercial, it was hate at first sight. Not only were the commercials in the series in outrageous taste, they failed to sell the product. They were trite, unbelievable, and executed childishly. On top of it all, they blatantly stated that there are some people, some families, who are better than others, and resorted to every distasteful stereotype in casting and every cheap trick available to show the differences.

Were the FTC truly concerned about us, it would dwell less upon the effects that cereals, disinfectants and throat lozenges have upon our bodies and more upon the possible effects of divisive, prejudiced dribble like this upon our minds and sensitivities.

This campaign for Colgate boils down to bad, unbelievable, stupid advertising. I wouldn't mind if the commercials had tried to convince me that the difference between the families was their toothpaste. Then it would have been merely silly and easy to dismiss as bad advertising. But that wasn't what they said. They really stated that there are some families who do everything right and others who do everything wrong, regardless of their toothpastes. The toothpaste was incidental to the basic theme line of the campaign: "Some families have it and some don't."

Commercials like this are not funny, and no comedy was intended. They were deadly serious. That's what upsets me. To be sure, the commercials were probably done by a well-meaning writer and art director, and nothing more insulting than selling the product (albeit badly) was meant. But advertising like this does harm to the whole business.

Every once in a while I pick on a campaign, only to find myself proved wrong. Take the Lufthansa Red Baron series. I've got to admit it: when this campaign first broke, I thought it was in lousy taste. I thought the idea of using a heavily accented, authoritarian German voice representing an arrogant military officer was pretty awful, because it was bound to conjure up all sorts of negative feelings in people who still remember World War II too well. It would be offensive to those who had suffered at German hands, I reasoned, and even today many Americans think of Germans as cold, efficient, arrogant, humorless robots. So why base a campaign on that?

Commercials that perpetuate ethnic stereotypes are the worst kind of bad taste advertising. Because sometimes the groans they elicit are real.

How easily these airline commercials could have fallen into the trap that almost made Hertz number zero with TV watchers all over the country! I'm talking about the Hertz commercial in which a German Gestapo agent takes us on a guided tour to show us Hertz's efficient operation. He winds up his sales speech by disclaiming responsibility for what goes on there: "I vos only following orders."

My God. If that one sent shivers down *my* back, you can imagine the effect it had on those who witnessed German efficiency firsthand not too long ago.

Almost anything I could say about this commercial would be in excess of the thunderclap of outrage its first few airings provoked. Needless to say, it was snatched off the air at once, never to resurface.

But the bad taste lingers. Which is why I was so leery of the first appearance of the Red Baron. The Red Baron—whether actual or fictitious I don't know—was a flying ace of World War I who came to stand for German efficiency in the air. It seemed a risky strategy, but as it turned out, I needn't have worried. I'm still sure that this Lufthansa campaign isn't a great one, and maybe it isn't even a good one, but it achieved at least one of its objectives—it sure put that airline on the map, and it did so in a very positive way.

Before this campaign broke, I was vaguely aware of Lufthansa, had a more negative than positive impression of it, and would never have considered flying it if I were offered a choice. Now the reverse is true. I know something about the airline, and it's all good.

The Red Baron theme is unique and exclusive to Lufthansa. That's its strength and it gives their commercials memorability. No other airline could use that theme, and in these days, when all airline advertising looks and sounds alike, this one stands out. Moreover, the Red Baron theme is coordinated beautifully in all media. The print ads, with their heavy Germanic typeface and Red Baron signature, are perfect adaptations of the TV logo, capturing the same feel, flavor, and look.

As for my misgivings about the campaign being in bad

taste, they evaporated because of the excellent treatment the Red Baron theme receives in many of the commercials. I think it was a wise decision to never visually present him. Instead, one gets to know him only through his voice and always as he relates to employees of his airline. He warns pilots not to go bump, bump, bump when they land, for example, because it spills the champagne. He informs the beautiful stewardesses that it has come to his attention that they are always smiling, laughing, and joking with passengers, and he, surprisingly, approves. He cautions mechanics to check, double-check and triple-check everything, and to be meticulous and methodical even when checking the champagne and caviar.

In all, these spots have made it impossible for me to think of the Red Baron as a Prussian, ex-Luftwaffe officer whose major delight was shooting down American planes. To me he is now a warm, pixie-like character with a sense of humor (though still an uncompromising, unrelenting perfectionist). As far as I'm concerned, the Red Baron's major happiness is now gained from running the world's most efficient airline when it comes to service and safety.

That's not a bad picture for people to have of an airline dealing with human lives. The German reputation for no-nonsense efficiency makes it all the more believable. So far from perpetuating a storm-trooper stereotype, this ad campaign has turned a negative image around into a strong, positive one. Those who still remember the war may not be convinced, but with no disrespect intended, I doubt they would ever fly Lufthansa anyway, with or without the Red Baron.

DOUBLE-ENTENDRE commercials created for their shock appeal are another example of bad taste that can hurt an advertiser's image. In a memo to his staff, John E. O'Toole, president of Foote, Cone & Belding, honed in on two specific examples. Air France's "Have you ever done it the French way?" campaign was one. These provocative lines are uttered in a provocative tone by a provocative bikini-clad girl in a provocative pose. The other campaign was Mennen's "Get off your can. Get on the stick" campaign for their underarm stick deodorant. Mr. O'Toole concluded his memo with this statement:

> The conventions of vaudeville dictated that when laughs weren't forthcoming, a sure way to bring the house down was for the comedian to drop his pants. Advertising, despite the misconceptions of a few, is not vaudeville. And a sale is more difficult to achieve than a laugh.

I agree, John, and a client's good name is more precious than a commercial.

So what can be done to guard against bad taste in advertising?

All who are charged with preparing or approving advertising, on the client side or agency, must always think first, before irreparable damage is done, of the company that is footing the bill. The single most important responsibility we who create advertising have, even more important than selling the client's product, is protecting his good name. The client's reputation is more important than all the creative advertising awards in the world. It's the client's name that is on the line, not our own, and though we may choose to take certain risks with our own reputations, we have no right to take any for him.

Bad taste in advertising may alienate a client's market from his product or cause the public to think less of him. That's why bad taste is the cardinal sin of advertising.

18

Untested Theories about TV Testing

AD PEOPLE, IT'S A FACT OF LIFE: SOMEDAY EVERY COMMER-
cial we put on the air will have been subjected to some sort
of test before, during, or after it appears on TV.

We'd better learn to live with this fact. Even if it makes us
feel like jurors who have been told that a verdict was reached
while we were out to lunch. Ad agencies will have to learn
to live with it, too. Because with commercial production
costs going up and up and the cost of air time rising, an
increasing number of advertisers are demanding proof that
their commercials are any good before they put a wad of
money behind them.

The problem is what kind of TV testing we can all live
with best. To me, the only really acceptable test is the one
at the cash register. We've all (eventually) got to accept that
one. The closest we can come to that is an in-market test in
which the client spends the money to produce the commercial, selects a test market where distribution is good, buys
time to run the commercial, and watches to see how it pays

off in the stores. Such a test, to my way of thinking, is the only really valid one.

But it's prohibitively expensive.

So what now? As a second choice, I could learn to live with any testing method that approximates an *in-store situation* involving an exchange of money. It sure beats the old pencil-and-paper type of research. What people *say* they'll do on a written questionnaire or to an interviewer can differ markedly from what they'll *actually* do in a store. People tend, for example, to react favorably to happy, entertaining commercials even though those commercials may be selling them nothing. By the same token they may react negatively to commercials that bring up unpleasant subjects but that do a heck of a job of selling at the same time.

Not so long ago I had the experience of watching one of the commercials I did turn in a so-so performance in group interviews and questionnaire testing—and then go on to break the bank on an in-store test. And I've had just the opposite happen, too. Which forces me to conclude that when it comes to actually spending their hard-earned money, consumers have no compunction about behaving in a manner totally opposite to the one they indicated on a pencil-and-paper survey.

I don't care at all about how people say they'll act, think they'll act, or would like me to believe they'll act in a buying situation. I only care about how they *do* act in the cash register line.

I don't believe in pencil-and-paper research; I only believe in dollar-and-cents research.

Theater testing is a popular technique where selected consumers are gathered in a theaterlike auditorium to watch commercials, either by themselves or mixed in with television pilot shows. They fail to produce valid statistics precisely because they are unreal situations. First of all, the audience is captive, and secondly, the audience associates the theater with entertainment and therefore responds better to entertaining commercials.

Nor do I trust "Man from U.N.C.L.E." devices. I've seen people turned into guinea pigs for TV testing, with their blood pressure, eye movements, perspiration, skin impulses, pupil dilations, brain waves, and even their dreams plotted and checked. I've seen people—sometimes through one-way mirrors—wired, cajoled, goaded, and psychoanalyzed. I've seen lie-detector tests. I've watched group therapy sessions on closed circuit television conducted by Ph.D.'s. I know all about bathroom flushometer tests (how many home toilets are flushed during commercial interruptions). And recently I heard of a testing method involving foot pedals.

All this in an attempt to find out whether people, consciously or unconsciously, like and respond to a given commercial. Now I'm not qualified to criticize any of these methods on scientific grounds. I don't necessarily like them or dislike them. In fact, I don't give a damn about any of them. All I care about is whether the commercial makes a buyer react favorably toward the product in a store. That's all. I don't care about people's unconscious feelings, or if these feelings are better clues than conscious reactions to the ways in which consumers will act at the check-out counter.

When discussing consumer reactions, the name of the game is not how, it's whether.

With that in mind, it's pretty hard for me to give much credence to any but on-air tests. There's no substitute for the privacy of the viewer's own living room, because there the viewer is king. He or she may not even *watch* the commercial, whereas in a test situation they're forced to watch. In all testing methods except on-air, the testers take for granted this most important of all factors for the success of a commercial: will it attract the attention of the viewer in the first place, so he'll actually watch it to the end?

Let me tell you some of the theories I've developed after years of open warfare against certain kinds of TV testing. The first theory begins with a strong hunch that most outstanding commercials will test poorly initially. People have a tendency to reject the unconventional, the unpredictable, the unknown, the daring, the challenging situations that make them feel uncomfortable. The challenge frightens them, so their reaction to it may be negative on a test even though the commercial may be selling them without their even knowing it.

Conversely, a benign and relatively harmless commercial will generally test well. If it's entertaining, all the better. Viewers will feel comfortable with it. Its predictability will invite recognition, and recognition invites a feeling of security. Familiar, logical, and nice-to-have-around as an old friend, a commercial like this is guaranteed not to grate or challenge or get anybody mad. It won't even make the viewer do any unpleasant work, like thinking. Soothing as a good sitz bath, your unimaginative commercial is bound to command a favorable reaction under test conditions.

I'm willing to bet two bits that many of the commercial concepts we consider successful today—both professionally and in dollars and cents—tested poorly at first. If agencies and advertisers had been gutless or had been shackled to testing evaluations, some of the era's best campaigns would have never seen the light of day.

And who knows how many never *did*?

Theory number two: Take those successful TV campaigns that tested so poorly the first time around. Test them again via the same method after they've been running on TV a while, say about six months, and see what happens to the scores. By this time the shock of unfamiliarity has worn off. The audience knows what to expect. They know the commercial. Feel comfortable with it. Accept it. And suddenly it leaves the pedestrian commercial that tested so well at the starting gate. Get the picture?

So where does that leave the advertiser who is about to spend thousands producing a commercial and millions running it? Isn't he entitled to know if the commercial is any good or not? Of course he is! And shouldn't he have the right to test the commercial? Of course he should! And won't some of the results of this test be helpful to the agency when it comes time to make another, stronger commercial? Of course they will!

All I'm saying is that an advertiser should take the results of any test as a guide, not as an absolute verdict. And finally, the commercial should be subjected to the most crucial test (and sometimes it's the most reliable test) of all: the test of *human intuition*—his own and his agency's.

I have one theory left, and this is it: the ones who succeed in advertising are the ones who know that making a *sale* rather than a high test score is the purpose of a commercial. The easiest thing a creative person can do is to construct a commercial that will score high using any given testing method. I can do it. So can any other creative person with half a brain. I've done it for a lark. Unfortunately, too many do it for a living.

In the end, even with our vast knowledge of how and why the human mind works, we just can't predict the behavior of others. For all the scientific gadgetry at our disposal, the most sensitive instrument for predicting the behavior of human beings is still the intuition of other human beings.

Thank goodness.

19

David Does
Goliath's Job

ONCE UPON A TIME WHEN EVERYONE WAS RICH AND AIR
time was less expensive, big-budget advertisers lavished
fistfuls of money upon their agencies for 60-second commercials. Today, the cost of both production and air time
for a 60-second commercial is prohibitive. So prohibitive
that these "long" commercials are used almost exclusively
for institutional or corporate-type commercials for huge
companies sponsoring documentary TV specials. Now
that the 60-second commercial is almost extinct, the 30-
second is king—for a while. I foresee the day when even the
30-second spot will go the way of all flesh and 20- and 10-
second spots will take its place.

Do the 10- and 20-second spots get squeezed to death
between those larger, Goliathan commercials? Are they
long enough to get a conceptual point across? Can these little
spots be used to introduce a new product? To make an
impression? To do something as specialized as registering a

new company name? Are they long enough to be remembered?

Or are they just a waste of time and money?

I began to formulate my opinions about short commercials the first time I saw one for the Bank of Commerce. I had never heard of that bank before. When the 20-second spot was over, though, I knew them as the "understanding" bank, which is a pretty nice reputation to have if you're a bank. Some banks spend 20 *years* instead of 20 *seconds* trying to establish a reputation like that.

The commercial? There were lots of them, all Lilliputian-sized. But the best of the lot featured a drawing of a man lying on a couch, seemingly in a psychiatrist's office. We see each of his dreams in idea balloons as they take shape—a building, a boat, a car. A soft-voiced announcer reassures the dreamer. Tells him not to worry, but to bring his dreams to the Bank of Commerce, where dreams have a way of coming true. The clincher is the line that tells us that the Bank of Commerce lends more than money. It lends understanding.

Nice? Neat? Simple? All of that and more. If I had to apply for a loan the day after I saw one of those spots, I think I'd start with the Bank of Commerce. And they convinced me on a comparatively tiny budget. (They didn't have to borrow from one of the big banks to pay for these commercials.)

In short (as it were), the little New York bank with the little spots stole the TV spotlight from such New York giants as First National City, Bankers Trust, Chemical, and Chase—all of whom can well afford 60-second commercials.

And just look at what a 10-second commercial can do! I'll bet your mother and grandmother and every professional painter you've ever seen used Soilax to wash down walls.

But how many newlyweds do you suppose would recognize that brand name? So Soilax set out to change all that with a short, sensible commercial that does the job. It just shows the storage area under the sink, where most people crowd their cleaning materials out of sight. Only *this* cupboard is bare except for a single box of Soilax. Before the cupboard is opened, an off-screen voice announces that "this kitchen cabinet contains a floor cleaner, a wall cleaner, a window cleaner, a sink cleaner, an oven cleaner, a comb and brush cleaner, . . ." All in less than 10 seconds. The point is obvious: the product is an all-purpose cleaner that takes the place of all that junk you keep under your sink.

Little David's slingshot strikes again.

Can a short spot do something more than just straightforward advertising? One did for the Oppenheimer Fund, which registered a new company, a new name, and a new corporate symbol in 10 short seconds. All it took was enough time for hands to grasp one another, forming the new logo. The name flashes upon the screen below the completed logo and wham-o! A visual image of the fund that's hard to forget is established.

I guess what all this is leading up to is a solid, unqualified endorsement of 10s and 20s. It's good to know that if you can't outspend your competition, you can still outsmart them. Even today.

You should know, though, that 10s and 20s pose a tremendous challenge to creative people. They challenge them to crystallize the single most important point they think should be made for a product. And that's good discipline for any creative person, even one with all the time in the world.

Short commercials are tough. You can't fake them. Any creative person who tries a 10- or 20-second commercial for the first time begins to understand at last the meaning of that old quip: "If I had more time, I'd write a shorter letter."

20
Marketing Quiz

THREE PRODUCTS ARE ABOUT TO COMPETE FOR THE SAME market. If any one of them can gain more than a 50 percent share, the rewards will be enormous. It will probably become the most famous, talked-about, and most successful product in the world. So famous that it might even change the course of the life of every American, and possibly every single person on earth.

The market these products are competing for is now wide open for a new brand in the category, and potential buyers include every male and female citizen of the United States over the age of 18. *Everyone* is a potential customer—rich and poor, young and old, industrialist and laborer, farmer, big city dweller, Easterner, Westerner, Northerner, Southerner.

The category? An essential product, a basic staple that everyone will buy in one of the three brands. And the customer will buy within the next couple of months.

It can't be stressed enough that, due to special circumstances, there is room for only one product to be marketed successfully in this category. Initial purchase is the essential objective. The surviving product can thrive very profitably on initial purchases for at least four years without the need for repeat orders.

Most important of all is the fact that the result of this marketing battle may well be determined by the products' exposure on TV.

Now then. If I give you some basic facts about each of the three brands and their histories, can you predict the outcome of the marketing battle?

OK, let's go. I've deliberately chosen a situation that's past history, so transport yourself back almost a decade in time.

Brand A: This is an old product that's been national since 1946. It reached its peak of popularity in 1960, when it came within a hair of becoming the country's leading brand in its category. But it didn't, and it slid badly after that.

Two years later, in 1962, a slightly improved product under the same name was test-marketed on a local basis. It failed again, and was taken out of distribution.

Secretly the company continued to revise and improve the product and to assure its distribution nationwide. Now, suddenly, it's been reinstated into the market with a tremendous budget behind it, and has managed to outsell other products made by the same company in test market battles across the country.

Faced with statistics like these, the company had no choice but to call back its other products and to go with Brand A. Today, Brand A is being marketed as a new and improved product. Distribution is excellent, with greatest potential strength in "B" and "C" markets—rural areas and the entire South.

Best of all, this brand has a good, professional marketing machine behind it and a seemingly inexhaustible budget with which it plans to make a pitch to suburbanites, special interest groups, executives, business leaders, professionals, and persons upscale in age and socioeconomic standing.

Special problems: Brand A has a reputation for being a loser. People distrust the product and find advertising claims made for it hard to believe. They remember the product's other failures and feel that they may be tricked if they buy this up-to-date version.

The product is weak in cities and with all minority groups, especially blacks. Nor is it particularly strong with laborers.

Brand A's problems might stem from the fact that it has a packaging problem and doesn't come across well on TV. Its new packaging is meeting with questionable success, and improvement is not readily apparent.

Brand B: This is the second product of a successful company whose first product recently had the leading brand in its category. This new product is a proliferation. Recently, share of their leading brand has slipped drastically, despite all efforts to protect its position. Accordingly, a decision was made several months ago to withdraw the slipping brand from the market and to prime Brand B for an attempt to capture the number one spot in that category for the company.

Brand B is not a new product. It's been around on the national marketing scene only two years less than Brand A, but no big money has ever been put behind it on a national scale.

Historically, it's been successful, but always on a local or regional basis. It was marketed nationally for the first time in 1964, but achieved distribution only by riding the coat-tails of the company's then-leading brand.

It has not been successfully test-marketed in various states as Brand A has, but at a recent meeting of the company's board of directors, representing all states, Brand B was the company's overwhelming choice to replace their quickly fading brand.

Distribution channels are excellent nationally, with particular strength in big city "A" markets. Strong in urban areas with people younger in age and lower on the socio-economic ladder than those of Brand A, this product can count on blue-collar purchasers in northern and eastern markets. It's also preferred by minority groups, but not overenthusiastically.

A good, professional marketing machine lies behind it, as well as a large advertising budget, which nevertheless still falls short of Brand A's funds.

Special Problems: The waning reputation and growing dissatisfaction with the company's leading brand may rub off on Brand B. It's no secret to the public that the same company makes both products, so it would prove embarrassing for Brand B to make advertising claims critical of the company's leading brand. Such claims would also be dangerous, since Brand B hopes to inherit the older brand's remaining loyal customers. Weak in the South, Bible Belt, and suburbia, the product still manages to come across well on TV.

Packaging seems adequate, if unspectacular.

Brand C: This is a new brand. It comes from an old-line company that's been around since the category's beginnings in regional markets. So far, it's met with varying degrees of success.

Brand C has one major thing going for it: the backing of a small but intensely loyal hard core of customers who are extremely well pleased with the product. Repeat purchase pattern is almost 100 percent.

But up till now, the brand has proved its strength in only one state. Predecessor brands by the same company have always managed to capture a steady one or two percent share—not a lot, but enough to stay in business. Recent research, however, pegs its current market potential anywhere between a 10 percent and 25 percent share nationally.

This brand has great strength in the South, with surprisingly strong (if spotty) support in the Mid and Far West. At this time, it's unclear whether this strength is coming at the expense of Brand A or Brand B. Research on this point is conflicting; Brand C can hurt both of the others, and may deprive either of them of better than a 50 percent share nationally, a percentage considered crucial to the success of Brand A or B.

In short, the product is an underdog, with little chance of capturing the largest share of the total market, though it may play the role of spoiler. By that I mean that Brand C hopes to make a good enough showing to prevent either Brand A or B from gaining a dominant share. In this way, Brand C hopes to get a good price for its company from the brand closest to winning and to have a loud voice in the running of the newly combined company.

Brand C has great strength with white, Anglo-Saxon Protestant customers, particularly in the South.

Special Problems: Distribution, while excellent in the South, is poor to nonexistent elsewhere. Just as consumers are extreme in their love of this product, those who do not like it are equally extreme in their dislike and will be very difficult (if not impossible) to win over. Conquest sales is its overall objective, so the product must develop a strategy that conquers sales from both Brands A and B, while building a strong, national brand awareness.

Brand C has a small, local marketing staff, inexperienced

in national marketing. It projects well on TV, but has had limited exposure. It operates on a comparatively small budget.

ALL right folks, those are the facts. Now can you guess the outcome of this marketing battle? Which brand do you think won the larger-than-50-percent share of market?

If you guessed Brand A, you guessed correctly.

And I'm sure you guessed something else, too. The examples cited above pertain to the biggest marketing battle of them all: the national presidential election. For the sake of argument, I chose the 1968 election because of the disparate personalities it involved: Nixon (Brand A), Humphrey (Brand B), Johnson (the slipping brand that Brand B was intended to replace) and Wallace (Brand C).

I can't really say, though, that things have been done very differently in the elections held since then. We're still selling candidates like soap or toothpaste (a fact my marketing quiz attempted to satirize), with the help of marketing specialists and advertising agencies. How the candidate looks, how he comes across on TV, even the way he does his hair has a great big bearing upon his electability.

And I don't think it should.

Do you really want a president whose rough spots have been so smoothed and virtues so glamorized that you don't know what you're "buying" when you vote?

Can you be absolutely certain that your vote wasn't influenced in this (or any) election by the "image" you saw on TV?

Indeed, did we elect a carefully orchestrated series of "images" to the White House, or a living, breathing man whom we knew well at the time we elected him?

You might be interested to hear the end of the marketing

quiz story. Four years after Brand A became the leader in its category, it was challenged again for the number one position. The most expensive advertising-marketing-public relations campaign of all time returned Brand A to the top for another four years.

The rest is history. The saddest chapter of our history, too.

So I really don't think candidates should be allowed to advertise. First, because the candidate with the largest budget has the greatest advantage. Second, because one may be more charismatic or more "advertisable" than the other, and charisma is hardly the same thing as leadership. Third, it's always possible that one candidate may hire a *better* advertising agency than the other. Which would get him elected because of a "better" public image projected. Which brings us full circle back to why I don't think candidates should be allowed to advertise at all.

I say no, because none of the above-named factors, which could determine the outcome of a very close race, have any bearing upon a candidate's qualifications for office.

I'm confirmed in this conviction when I consider the consequences of unlimited peddling of political images. I don't mind making a mistake when I buy a bar of soap or a shaving cream or a meatball. As long as they're not harmful, how much have I lost by buying them one time? But making a mistake when spending my vote—that's something else again. I can't return the "purchase" or obtain a better substitute within 10 days. And the "product" bought may turn out to be harmful after all. Very *very* harmful.

Nor would I, as an advertising man, mind making a mistake when selling that bar of soap or shaving cream. Mistakes happen. Advertising agencies often find that the public doesn't like the product as much as the agency did. So the product is quietly withdrawn from the market and the agency chalks it up to experience, a luxury an ad man can't afford when he's helped foist an underqualified candidate upon the public. When you're selling the President, the stakes are too high to allow a margin for error. And that's why I think no one should sell the President at all.

Candidates should sell themselves.

This is not to say that the miracle of mass communications should be ignored; its potential for good is just too great. I do think, though, that all media should be required to donate equal space or time to *all* of the candidates, allowing them to confront each other publicly on the issues. Imperfect as this solution would be (a dynamic personality and glib delivery will always sway voters), it would at least be a step in the right direction. And some would argue—rightly so, I think—that a dynamic personality and glib delivery are almost prerequisites for the job of President, anyhow.

In any case, it would be a whole lot fairer. Then advertising could get back to its real vocation: selling products and services instead of people.

21

The Regulation of TV Advertising

LET ME COME RIGHT TO THE POINT.

The day is fast approaching when the only thing an advertiser will be able to say about his product on TV is its name, its function, and where it can be bought.

Mind you, I understand the reason for the existence of self-regulatory bodies. I even agree with the purpose they're supposed to serve. But when the creative directors of agencies complain that their best commercials are being turned down or watered down, it's time to take another look at these regulatory bodies.

First of all, which agencies are complaining? Are they the charlatans, hucksters, wheeler-dealers, and marginal operators of the business? They are not. I'm talking here about the most respected and admired agencies, the most reputable advertisers.

Ed McCabe, highly respected creative partner in one of the most highly respected advertising agencies of the seventies, Scali, McCabe, Sloves, had this to say to *The New York Times Magazine* recently regarding a commercial his agency was making for a client, Hebrew National hot dogs: "The networks are our biggest problem. . . . You've got to document every goddam comma. All you need is a confrontation with the networks to send you screaming to the booby hatch." Dick Roth, management supervisor at the same agency, complained in the same article: "You get a different response from each one. One accepted it [the commercial], one said you've got a problem, and one said you're commercializing God—that's a no-no. They set standards for taste and morality in the ads and they destroy those standards in their programming."

What do agencies mean by "watered down"? Generally speaking, they feel that the regulatory bodies have a tendency to lean over backwards in the direction of playing it safe. That's understandable, if not especially desirable. But agencies are also saying that these regulatory bodies are becoming more and more arbitrary in their interpretation of their own regulations. No matter how sound those regulations are by themselves, that's bad. In many cases, what you *can* do on television is separated from what you *can't* do by such a thin line as to challenge credibility. What's worse, the line has been known to waver. Agencies are saying that some of the decisions they're being handed are downright silly, and finally, that standards vary from regulatory body to regulatory body. And that's the worst of all.

An agency with a drug or health account is not going to screech about close scrutiny when it's applied to the claims they make for the product. They know as well as anyone that the direct effect the product is likely to have upon the public's well-being makes such scrutiny necessary.

I'm talking about products that do not affect the public

health in such an immediate way, about their use of claims that do *not* involve out-and-out lies, exaggerations, weasels, or impossible-to-substantiate statements.

I'm talking about truths that can be proved.

Truth and honesty in advertising are desirable goals. So desirable that I'm campaigning for more truth. The full truth. If a product has a provable advantage over a competitor's, I feel that product's advertising should be entitled to tell that truth, even if someone else's product is hurt by it.

Someone is always hurt by the truth. That's how it should be.

I'm vigorously opposed to any attempt by regulating bodies to remove all trace of competitiveness from commercials. That would be a shame. It's removing the guts from advertising. The challenge. The bite. And much of the results. And, more important, it's depriving the public of all the facts they are entitled to know.

To me, the whole objective of advertising is to prove to the public that your product is better than your competitor's. The most effective commercial I can imagine is one that says: "Here is my product, here's my competitor's product; now let me show you why mine is better." To a limited degree, we have this situation developing now in a few television commercials. I think we'll see more of it as advertisers realize that if what they say is true and able to be proved to the satisfaction of a regulatory board, they should *have* the right and *use* their right to make and run this type of commercial.

What do the regulatory bodies say about the use of direct comparison in TV commercials? The TV Code Review Board "urges advertising to offer products or services on their positive merits, and to refrain from discrediting, disparaging, or unfairly attacking competitors, competing products, other industries, professions, or institutions." The American Association of Advertising Agencies, as quoted by the National Association of Broadcasters, says that "although it believes in competition in advertising . . . it does not believe in advertising which untruthfully or unfairly depicts or disparages competitive products or services." Agreed.

But I would hope that both of these august bodies would defend to their dying breaths the kind of advertising that *truthfully* and *fairly* depicts a difference between products. If advertisers allow advertising to be stripped of its most potent weapon—the demonstration of a product's advantage over competitive products—they will have only themselves to blame when the day arrives that they'll be permitted to give only the name, rank, and serial number of their clients' products on television. And then there will no longer be the kind of advertising we all believe in, the kind that built brands and giant companies from nothing, the kind that permits a new company with a great new product to take on the giants and beat them. In fact, it won't be advertising at all. And this will no longer be the business I want to be in.

We—not just advertising people, but all of us in a free society—have an obligation to fight *unfair* competition wherever it crops up. But we have an equal obligation to vigorously defend *fair* competition and to protect the medium in which it can flourish. That brings me to the point I think some of our regulatory bodies are missing: In the final analysis, the public has the right to know the true and complete facts before it chooses between products. Doesn't it? Advertisers have the right to benefit from their ingenuity in developing better products, don't they? And the ad man has the right to decide when, where, and how he will tell the public about the product in the strongest possible way, doesn't he?

Or does he?

When cigarette commercials were banned from the airwaves I spoke out to castigate the government for that decision because it usurped the advertiser's right to select where he shall advertise. I also said that the public, not the government, should be the judge of a product's merits, and that the decision to remove cigarette advertising from TV showed a complete lack of faith in the intelligence of the American people. I still think so. If cigarettes are as harmful as they say, and the government is so concerned with the health of its citizens, then why didn't it have the guts to go all the way and prohibit the manufacture of cigarettes altogether? I would have respected them for that. Instead, the government continues to accept with no trace of reluctance the taxes derived from cigarettes and eases its conscience by banning cigarette advertising from the often violence-racked TV tube.

Be honest: Did the censorship imposed by the Federal Communication s Commission actually stop people from smoking? Or, more important, did it stop youngsters from starting? Not on your life! Does the absence of hard liquor advertising on TV stop alcoholism? And marijuana and heroin have done quite well without TV advertising, thank you.

The simple fact is that the "Big daddy must protect us from ourselves" philosophy is not only alien to us, it's also ineffective. It doesn't really discourage the use of the forbidden product. And where will it end? If a restriction is placed on one product, others are endangered. Putting it another way, if a government agency can ban the advertising of a legal product in a particular medium (And why it should be banned in one medium and not in another I'll never know. Do they think that kids and cigarette smokers don't see newspapers, magazines, and posters? Maybe they think they can't read.), what is to stop the government from banning advertising of other legal products? After all, some detergents are pollutants. They could be next. Or deodorant or mouthwash or beer or anything for any number of reasons!

In today's marketing, television advertising can spell the difference between life or death for a product. Which regulatory body has the right to play God?

I'm certain that all the regulatory boards, both governmental and industry related, would disclaim any desire to play God, insisting instead that they're only doing a job that advertising agencies should be doing for themselves: putting concern for public welfare before concern for one's pocketbook in choosing the advertisers whose message will reach millions via TV advertising. The clear implication in sermons like these is that if we advertising agencies were less greedy, the need for such regulatory bodies would not exist.

Bull!

Let me point out that a couple of agencies publicly refused to handle a cigarette account well before the product was banned from TV. So much for the greedy theory.

However, what these agencies lack in greed they make up for in hypocrisy. I hasten to point out that while these same pious defenders of the American consumer were curling their corporate lips at cigarettes, they thought nothing of handling automobile accounts whose defective safety equipment has the potential to kill and maim a helluva lot more of our citizens than cigarettes will.

These same agencies see nothing wrong with preparing advertising for toothpaste when all dental authorities tell us that brushing with water is just as effective. They sell soft drinks so full of sugar as to rock our metabolic systems. They sell milk and cream and bacon, all of which play havoc with our cholesterol counts. They advertise franks as "all meat" when they're mostly fat. And they help move ethical drugs which are priced 50-100 times higher than they ought to be.

Look, I'm not condemning these agencies for handling accounts like these, I just condemn their hypocrisy. A couple of years ago, for example, a large agency resigned a cigarette account because they were just placing the advertising in media and not being paid to create it. The story they put out to cover themselves was that they no longer felt comfortable with a cigarette account. Doing the creative work, it is assumed, would have made them feel so much more at ease. This is what I mean by hypocrisy.

Would I handle a cigarette account? Absolutely, even though I gave up smoking many years ago. Our citizens have been bombarded over the last five to ten years with information about the hazards of cigarette smoking. It's been in all the newspapers, in all the magazines, on all the radio and TV stations of the nation in the single greatest campaign ever launched against anything. And just in case anyone missed the message, it's stated again on every cigarette package every smoker picks up at least twenty times. If, in the face of the evidence, an adult, knowing full well the hazards associated with cigarette smoking, nevertheless makes the decision to smoke, who has the right to tell him he can't? And, so long as he's going to smoke, I want him to smoke my brand.

So what does that mean to the regulatory bodies?

It means that the time is ripe for them to rethink the whole concept of free enterprise. That "truth in advertising" means the *whole* truth, not just that portion of it that doesn't embarrass anyone else. It means that forbidding a legal product access to an advertising medium amounts to outright censorship and constitutes an infringement upon that advertiser's rights as well as the public's right to choose.

It means Big Brother go home.

22
Advertising Awards: The Envelope Please

IF YOU'VE GATHERED THUS FAR THAT I DON'T AGREE WITH the idea of competition for advertising awards, you're right. I think they're nonsense that reduces the credibility of the business to the level of Hollywood.

The advertising business is a profession practiced (I hope) by professionals. At least we'd like to think of ourselves as professionals. If doctors and lawyers manage to survive without awards competitions, why can't we? Can you imagine doctors giving awards for Best Appendectomy of the Year, or lawyers for Best Landlord-and-Tenant Litigation of the Year?

Doctors and lawyers don't announce the acquisition and loss of patients and clients publicly, with great fanfare, as we do. We allow gossip sheets and half-baked imitation Walter Winchell columnists to exist, and even court their favor. Is that professional?

And how about the Hall of Fame for both copy and art.

We've got to be kidding! What egomaniacs we are, so obsessed with our own self-importance. Let's put what we do in perspective. We're not engaged in the fight against cancer. We don't alleviate human suffering. We don't pursue great humanitarian causes. None of us will ever win a Nobel Peace Prize, or even beat Hank Aaron's home-run record. I'm not belittling what we do. I'm proud of what we do. But in the context of mankind, let's stop getting carried away with ourselves and forget this Hall of Fame nonsense. If we *must* have our little pats on the head, let's do it right by holding one big award competition in which the winners are picked seriously, not by laugh meter.

The forced gag is almost a prerequisite to winning an award. As a result, you can hardly watch a TV commercial or listen to a radio commercial anywhere that isn't based on a gag, a joke, a pun, a comedy routine, a capsulized situation comedy, a skit, or, at the very least, a closing yak.

Surely laughter can't be the only way to attract people, to stir them, to move them to action. There must be other ways, like honesty, simplicity, believability, conviction. Is humor the bribe we offer our prospects so they'll buy our products?

I am certainly not against humor in advertising, with these restrictions:

1. It must not get in the way of the message.
2. It must be functional to the sale of the product.
3. It must help to make sales points, not obscure them.
4. It must be compatible with the nature of the product.

Humor can be a dangerous weapon in unskilled hands. It can also be a great and valuable tool of advertising.

But it's not the only effective tool.

The day has finally arrived when advertisers are looking at the numbers and finding that the smiles don't add up. That there is not necessarily a direct correlation between smiles and sales, between the laugh register and the sales register.

That selling a funny commercial to a client may be easier than selling a serious product to a prospect.

After all, you know why so many "funny" commercials reach the air, don't you? For two reasons: funny commercials win awards and funny commercials represent the easy way out. A skit is easy to sell a client because when the agency presents it to the ad manager, he smiles; and when the ad manager presents it to the president, *he* smiles; and when the president presents it to the chairman, *he* smiles; and when the chairman presents it to his wife, *she* smiles; and when neighbors and fellow country club members compliment the company's officers on their entertaining commercials, the whole world smiles.

But people don't buy products because they find the commercial *amusing*. They buy products because they find the commercial *convincing*.

And I find very few of the award-winning commercials from the past few years to have been convincing. So let's stop creating commercials to please awards committees and keep in mind what a commercial is supposed to do: it's got to convince someone who is not using your product to try it once, for a believable reason. If the people who create commercials would think of themselves as consumers and ask themselves, "If I am using a competitor's product, would this commercial I'm doing convince me to try this other product?"—we'd see more and better reasons for trying the products advertised on TV.

What's more, if all advertising people were *completely* honest with themselves, I wonder how many of the award-winning commercials would have been run in the form in which we saw them? I can't believe the creators of Rambler's "Driving Lesson" commercial would themselves buy a

Rambler because they saw a snickery sequence of comedy. Nor would anyone from the agency that created the zillion-dollar Contac "Cold Diggers" commercial buy the product on the basis of what they learned from it.

And nobody, not even Alka-Seltzer's own agency, is going to assuage a sick stomach with Alka-Seltzer instead of a tried-and-true brand just because George Raft banged his cup against a table in a prison mess hall.

No, if we're going to go on giving ourselves awards, we are obliged to give awards to the very best we can turn out. To the kind of commercials that sell. To the execution that crystallizes the concept best. To the copy that gives us the best switching idea.

To insure this, we must pick the most qualified people to judge and the best method of judging. I've seen too many of these judging sessions turn into a good time for all. I've seen too many popularity polls, too much jealousy, too much bitchiness. And too many biased juries and jurors who all think the same way.

No system for judging commercials is foolproof, but certainly the way we're doing it today can't be right.

Nor can this overproliferation of ceremonies and award-granting organizations be right, either.

Some shows give so many awards, for so many things, to so many people, almost everyone wins something. (The more winners, of course, the more tickets sold.) Besides the winning commercial, there are four or five runners-up, plus four or five more "recognitions" in every category from Apparel to Utilities. As if that wasn't enough, there are further awards that get almost as silly as best performance by a male schnauzer in a 30-second dog-food commercial. And these awards are judged by a jury of thousands nobody's ever heard of, most of whom, by my standards, are not qualified to judge anything more serious than a beauty contest. The latest wrinkle in awards is actual cash prizes instead of medals or statuettes. How mercenary can they get.

On the positive side, I'd like to compliment the American Marketing Association on its Effie award, which seems to have more sense to it than most. This association demands that each entry be accompanied by a marketing strategy, objective, and documented proof of its success before it can be considered for an award. That makes good sense, because it's really awfully silly to give an award for advertising excellence to an ad that failed to sell the product. Unfortunately, the Effie awards are not as popular as some of the others. I'm not sure why, unless it's because all those show biz whizzes never heard of a marketing strategy. Maybe they couldn't figure out the objective of some of their nonobjective creations. Or maybe, just maybe, they had a hard time documenting the success of some of the stuff that's been collecting the fancy hardware at all those Hollywood orgies run by the other award shows.

Agencies pay through the nose for these shows: entry fees, hanging fees, and tables for themselves and their clients at all the awful luncheons and dinners where the food is terrible and the service worse. Nobody really enjoys them, but everybody's afraid to miss them. I haven't been to one in ten years and I don't miss them at all.

If advertising creative people are so childish and insecure as to require the security blanket of awards, at least let's cut them down to one. That would be bearable, and awards might take on meaning again.

Or best of all, let's lionize the advertising person's only real award: the knowledge that his or her ad sold the product. I think Al Hampel of Benton & Bowles said it best in his now-famous line, "It's not creative unless it sells."

In the last analysis, that's the only award that really counts.

23
A Simple Business

"When you take away the exposés, the psychology, the personalities, the textbooks, and the rules, what have you got left? This book!"

. . . a short book, because I have just told you everything I know about advertising. I don't know anything more. But, then again, as I warned you at the very beginning, I'm a "Simplifier." I feel certain that somewhere within these pages you will find an answer to any question or any problem you may come across relating to the creation of advertising.

See, advertising is really a simple business. Pure and simple. Don't let anyone tell you it's complicated. It's so simple, in fact, it's hard. Very hard. It has destroyed many, but if you like it, it will hold you lovingly in its grasp for the rest of your days—to say nothing of nights.

I love it.